More Praise for *Making Your Net Work*

"*Making Your Net Work* is a great read for anyone in business. In his book, Billy Dexter and Melissa G Wilson outline the common networking mistakes most business professionals make and the often-hidden ways the power players get ahead. But it's not just about getting ahead. Billy and Melissa show you how you can benefit by helping others, by being a generous person. The book is easy to read, and full of actionable advice. I recommend it!"

— **Andy Friedman**
Chief Content Officer
American Marketing Association

"Billy and Melissa do a masterful job combining decades of experience into succinct strategies for individuals at all levels willing to improve their networking capabilities. Blending science and art is often difficult, however, they make the case for stronger networking and then bravely use their personal journeys as a backdrop to demonstrate real application of business networking; a refreshing approach.

These networking luminaries shared secrets into how to strategically build, grow and incorporate networking into everyday life — attributing a focus on helping others as being their true North."

— **Van B Sapp**
Vice-Chairman, Southeast Management Advisory Group, LLC
Adjunct Professor, Concordia University Chicago, College of Business

"Great Work! *Making Your Net Work* highlights the importance of creating a networking Brand. Billy & Melissa are amazing connectors!"

— **Stedman Graham**
Author/Speaker S. Graham & Associates

"Valuing relationships and creating connections that matter are critical for personal & Career Success. *Making Your Net Work* is a must read for those looking to create a game plan."

— **DE Maurice Smith**
Executive Director of NFL Players Association

"*Making Your Net Work* makes it clear how to get in the game and make connections that will make you an impact player! Billy is a true master at creating relationships with a very authentic style. How you execute your best play is brilliant!"

— **Byron Spruell**
President NBA Basketball Operations

"*Making your Net Work* helps you create a blue print for personal & career success. Billy & Melissa have created an amazing book that outlines the Art & Science of Networking while also sharing their personal journeys. Well done and I will recommend to family, friends, and clients."

— **Tom Moran**
Managing Partner / Heidrick & Struggles

"What a refreshing look at a process for how to network. Billy & Melissa gift to us *Making Your Net Work* helps to bridge the gap by providing insights on how to integrate networking into your lifestyle."

— **Sheila Talton**
CEO Gray Matter Analytics

MAKING YOUR NETWORK

Mastering the Art and Science of Career and Business Networking

BILLY DEXTER
MELISSA G WILSON

MAKING YOUR NET *WORK*

Mastering the Art and Science of Career and Business Networking

by Billy Dexter and Melissa G Wilson

ISBN: 978-1-944027-06-3

Copyright © Networlding Publishing, 2017
All Rights Reserved

www.networlding.com

Dedication

In memory of my parents, Eddie Bill Dexter and Marion Mickey Dexter, and sisters, Eddie Jean and Brenda Lynn, and older brother, Leon Butch Dexter, who were always so supportive and provided me unconditional love throughout my journey. I take you everywhere with me.

To my wife, Gisel, and my two daughters, Alissa and Alexis, who give me life and make me want to "Live Our Best Lives Together." Also a special dedication to my younger brother, Pastor Michael Dexter, who has been the rock of our family and my personal hero and has been on this journey with me all his life.

To my extended family of aunts, uncles, cousins, nieces, and nephews—all I ever wanted in life was to be someone you could be proud of and be a role model for you. This book is dedicated to our family's journey.

- Billy D

To Billy, for creating so much good in the world with his networks. To the many wonderful people who have helped me throughout these years, filled with both struggle and success. Finally, to the strongest supporter of my network, my husband, Craig.

- Melissa

TABLE OF CONTENTS

INTRODUCTION
The Art and Science of Networking...............13

CHAPTER 1
Finding Your Success Lane..............17
Your turn: Take the networlding assessment.................20

CHAPTER 2
Working Your Net..23
Questions about networking...25
You can't get there from here..26
A relational vs. transactional approach........................28
You *can* get there from *here*..**29**
The levels of effective networking..30
    LEVEL 1: *Traditional networking*..30
    LEVEL 2: *Strategic networking*..30
    LEVEL 3: *Mentoring, strategic alliances, partnering*......................30
    LEVEL 4: *Sponsorships*..31
    LEVEL 5: *Connection hubs*..31
Exploring networking further..33

The networking knowledge gap 34
How do you feel about networking? 35

CHAPTER 3
Ten Reasons Why People Dislike Networking 37

1. Feeling awkward 37
2. Not knowing who to approach 39
3. Not knowing what to say 40
4. Fearing rejection 41
5. Feeling pressured 42
6. Feeling like a pest 42
7. Having trouble keeping track of contacts 43
8. Not always feeling up to it 44
9. Believing that networking is a waste of time 44
10. Feeling dirty 45

CHAPTER 4
Create Value for Those in Your Network 47

Initiating value-based relationships by telling your story. 52

CHAPTER 5
Strategic Networking 59

Strategic networking starts with building a values-based personal brand 61
Trust and strategic networking 62

Find points of commonality.. 67
Achieving a quality network... 70
Quantity vs. quality.. 72

CHAPTER 6
What Do Great Networks Look Like? 75

The power of creating your own network 75
Taking your network to the next level through unique connections 77
Adapting to change 78
Creating connection hubs 80

CHAPTER 7
Building Your Brand and Your Brand Story....85

Reflections and pointers 91
Building my brand story.. 92
A turn of events 95
Creating one of my first networks that built my brand..... 97
Show how your networking brand will help others........... 99
How to develop your networking brand 100
How are you introduced? 101

CHAPTER 8
Execute Your Best Play.. 105

Will's best play 107
Manage how you show up: Dress for success.................. 109
Finding your best play 111

CHAPTER 9
The Art of Building Your Network 113

Be here now 114
The art of possibility 117
Keeping an optimistic outlook creates connection opportunities 118

CHAPTER 10
The Science of Making Your Net *Work* 123

Networlding Support Exchange 124
Initiate a support exchange 126
    Emotional support questions 126
    Informational support questions 127
    Knowledge support questions 127
    Promotional support questions 128
    Wisdom support questions 128
    Transformational opportunities questions 129
    Bonus questions 129
How Melissa built her network 131
Networking facilitation 141
A growing concern: Adult loneliness 143

CHAPTER 11
Create a Robust Networking Strategy 147

One-on-one vs. group networking 151
Developing a networking plan and timeline 152
Local vs. national 154

Formal networks 155
Short-term vs. long-term strategies 156
Your target list 159

CHAPTER 12
Use Social Media to Create Connections that Matter 161

High tech and high touch 162
Branch out 162
Helping your net **work** with LinkedIn 163
    Start with your profile 164
    Ask to connect 164
    Use InMail 165
    Consider upgrading your account 165
    Take a course on how to use LinkedIn 166
    Engage with your community 166
    Tests and certifications 166
    Stay active 167
Helping your net **work** with Facebook 167
    Be conscious 167
    Don't brag 168
    Look for how you can serve 168
    Discover what your connections care about 169
    Engage 169
    Join groups 169
Helping your net **work** with Twitter 170
    Decide what you want to talk about 170
    Create a strong profile 170
    Follow people you want to get to know 171

Use it to go local.. *171*
Helping your net ***work*** with emails and texts................... 171

CHAPTER 13
Become a Network Thinker 173
Bringing it home... *176*

CHAPTER 14
Integrate Networking into Your Everyday Life 181
Maintaining your network... *185*
Commencement *193*
Before you go... *198*

ABOUT THE AUTHORS 199
Billy Dexter...199
Melissa G Wilson 200

ACKNOWLEDGEMENTS... 203
by Melissa 203
by Billy 204

NETWORKING TIPS 205

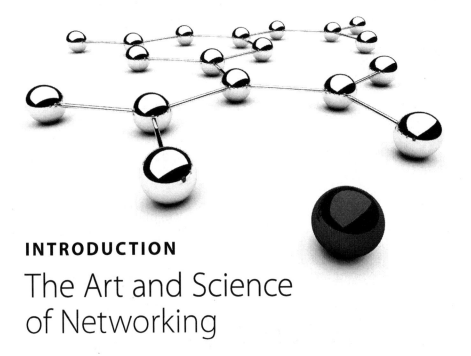

INTRODUCTION
The Art and Science of Networking

In this book, Melissa and I share how we developed our networking mindsets, philosophies, strategies, and tactics to help you understand that you can start wherever you are today, and like us, build a network to support a more successful career or business.

But, perhaps even more importantly, Melissa and I share our very personal stories of our respective paths to mastering the art (that would be me) and the science (that would be Melissa) of networking. Throughout this book we will be as transparent as possible about our back stories--those stories that really show the reasons why we chose to take one fork in the road rather than another. So, before we get going, here is more about the professional paths we took to get to where we are today.

Melissa has spent decades teaching networking to thousands of people. Her most recent book, *Networking Is Dead: Making*

Connections that Matter, was a *Wall Street Journal* and Barnes and Noble bestseller and her book *Networlding: Building Relationships and Opportunities for Success* was a #10 seller on Amazon for an entire year. She has taught networking at companies including Motorola, American Express, and Office Depot, as well as in smaller organizations across the country. She also uses her networking skills to help nonprofits, socially responsible organizations, and, currently, her own nonprofit mentoring initiative focused on helping the next generation get better starts in their careers and lives.

If anyone knows networking, it's Melissa. That's why I asked her to co-author this book. Like me, she's a natural networker, but she's also brought in the science of networking, making it easier to replicate.

Melissa developed her networking skills to create a great new career path for her life. To this end, I remember, during one of our book-writing sessions when I was telling her how my work matches well with my personal passion and skills around networking. I also shared with her that I recognized the similar strengths she had in networking, but, even more so now, in helping others write books.

I remember seven years ago when she transitioned from writing her own books to helping others write their books. She started with hosting writers' workshops, one of which I attended and where I got to see her use her writing and coaching skills first-hand. I knew I wasn't ready to write my book then, but she patiently waited for me until I was ready and, over the past two years, we've worked to join our respective experiences, research, insights, and practices together to write this book. Today, Melissa is indeed in her success lane, leveraging her strengths with her network. And, similarly, my clients are a key part of my network, a network where I am constantly strategizing how I can help them.

Similarly, networking has become an integral part of the work I do every day as an executive recruiter. Currently I'm a partner at Heidrick and Struggles, a worldwide executive search firm. My personal brand here is that I am a connector. At Heidrick, we help our clients change the world, one leadership team at a time. To this end we are hired to find leadership talent for other organizations. For our firm, being successful is about finding, developing, and sustaining the *best relationships*.

In my world making connections and developing relationships are critical in connecting executive level talent to strategic leadership roles for our clients. Having great relationships and a vibrant network equals currency in talent acquisition.

Now, together, Melissa and I are very excited to help you build your own success lanes, something we both know comes from developing your networking skills. This starts with tapping into both the art and science of networking. Whether you are just starting out in your career or business or have years under your belt, we are confident that the strategies, tactics, tips and stories we offer throughout this book, will help you take your networking to new levels of success. But before we begin, let me share with you my story to help you get to know me, part of the process we have found is essential to building a successful network.

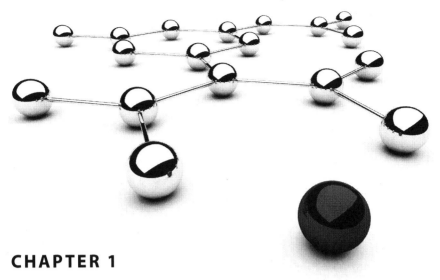

CHAPTER 1

Finding Your Success Lane

"It's been twenty-seven years since you graduated. It's time to tell your story, Billy." Those are the words my brother Michael said to me the night I told him I'd been asked to return to Saginaw Valley State University to be honored with their Outstanding Alumni Award. The invitation got me thinking back to a time in my life before I started on my career path, a path that has brought so many blessings to me and my family, friends, and colleagues. It took me back to when I was growing up in inner-city Detroit with Michael and my mom, back when I didn't know what I would do with my life.

Michael is only ten months younger than I, and we are pretty close. Mom had been divorced from my father since I was thirteen. Life was a constant struggle for her, a single mother working to support two boys, who had already raised three other siblings who no longer lived at home. But it was still a shock to me—a moment I've thought about again and again—when she brought Michael and I together one day, sat us down on her bed, put her arms around us, and said, "Mommy will take care of you two until you're eighteen. Then, you're on your own. You'll be men at eighteen and then you'll be on your own."

So as I neared my eighteenth birthday, with my senior year coming to an end, I started to give some thought to college, even though no one in my family had gone to college. In fact, no one in my family had even entertained the idea of going. My parents, my two older sisters, and my older brother hadn't even graduated high school. But I had hopes. They were small hopes, but they were hopes nonetheless. Those hopes pushed me to keep trying, to search for something better for myself and for the people whose lives I would impact. I thought, "Why not me?" It was those hopes that led me to Saginaw Valley State University, a small, liberal arts school in a rural community about two hours north of Detroit.

All these years later, I was nervous about accepting the award because it meant I would have to confront my past. Even though the past had been very positive and transformational for me, I had buried it, never planning to revisit it. So when I thought about going back, my mind returned to that seventeen-year-old kid who was trying to make something happen. I was graduating from high school and, although I had applied to sixteen schools, they had all turned me down, basically saying I was not college material. But one rejection letter, the one from Saginaw Valley—ended with an offer for me to contact them if I would like to discuss their decision further. That's when I made one of the most critical decisions of my life by skipping school one day, catching a ride with a friend, leaving inner-city

Detroit for the first time, except for a couple of church retreats in Brighton, Michigan, and driving up to Saginaw.

As I thought about going back there, I was extremely nervous. "Mike," I said to my brother, "I'm scared to death. I don't know if I can do this. I don't want to revisit this." He replied, upbeat, "Billy, we are so proud of you!" And then he added, solemnly, "Listen, God gave you those experiences so you could help other people. You've been out living those experiences. You've been humbled by them. That's why you've been blessed by them. You've been given these experiences for a reason. Stop running from this. Embrace it. It's time to tell your story."

My story is really about the journey I've taken that has led me to understand who I am—that I am a connector. I am an individual who embraces the power of networking not just to help myself, but more importantly, to help other people. That is my success lane. I'll share more of that story with you later in this book. For now, let me invite you into my journey to help you if, like me, you've struggled with finding the lane you're supposed to be in, your "success lane," as I mentioned above. Come along if you want to learn how to make networking work for you.

Your turn: Take the networlding assessment

Throughout this book we'll provide you with both the process (the science) and the creative nuances (the art) of networking that we've developed over time. These strategies, tactics, tips, and examples will help you create vibrant, sustainable networks. But before we go into all that detail, here's an exercise that will help you discover your own beliefs and preconceptions about networking. It was developed by Melissa as part of what she calls "networlding," a process we'll discuss in the next chapter.

Retake this quiz periodically to see how you change, or if you change. Be honest. No one will see this but you. Use this assessment to identify and address the specific gaps you have in your current networking efforts. This will help you as your read this book.

	Never = 1	Seldom = 2	Sometimes = 3	Often = 4	Always = 5
I believe it's important to make a difference.					
I believe anything is possible.					
I believe I am guided by strong inner beliefs, intent, or principles.					
I believe in partnering with others.					
I believe that with great networking partners I can get powerful results.					
I believe people are my most creative resource.					
I share my goals with my networking partners.					
I build and nurture relationships with my networking partners.					
I limit relationships with selfish individuals and those who don't help me realize my goals.					
I respect the creative process of networking.					
I believe that good networking shortens the time to achieve my goals.					
I assume that good networking is a balanced process of giving and asking for support.					
I believe that good networking can help me achieve most of my goals.					
When networking, I ask for what I need or want.					
When networking, I work to discover the interests and needs of those with whom I network.					
When networking, I expect to discover and create new opportunities for myself and my networking partners.					
I network with people who can regularly make introductions.					
I offer emotional support, informational support, and other support to my networking partners.					
I respond quickly to the requests and needs of my networking partners.					
I measure the results of networking efforts.					
Total your score:					

Score: novice 20–44, networker 45–64, strategic networker 65–84, networlding expert 85–100

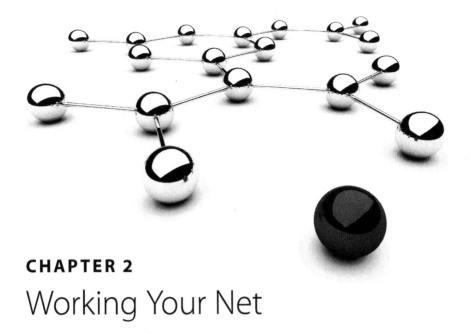

CHAPTER 2

Working Your Net

We use the metaphor of a "net" in this book to explore the principles of creating a successful network. We've capitalized the *N* in net and the *W* in work in the book's title to emphasize this idea. Begin by visualizing your own net and how you use it to build one significant connection after another. It's important to note the value of every connecting point in your network.

Over the last twenty-plus years, Melissa and I have built networks that have truly changed our lives for the better, and more importantly, had a positive impact on the lives of others. Through our connections, we've developed a networking process that has nurtured us and brought us to the point where we want to help others reach the kinds of successful outcomes that we've achieved.

Together, we'll give you an insider's view of networking effectively. How? By showing you both the *art* and the *science* of the process, and by teaching you how to differentiate between the two. We'll also show you how to balance the art and the science to get the most out of every networking situation and to help you develop a significant and rewarding career path.

For the past two decades, Melissa's focus has been on the *science* of building successful networks. I see my process as more *art*—creative and intuitive—something I do naturally. After two years of spirited conversations during our writing sessions, I came to realize that I am also very intentional (scientific) when building networks. Melissa points out that I'm *strategic* rather than manipulative, which is something she's also conscious of herself.

What we mean when we say *strategic* is that we are *awake in our networks*. That means we consciously build our connections by:

- Making time to meet new people.
- Listening deeply and asking probing questions.
- Looking for connection points, whether commonalities, mutual interests, or people we have in common. Creating this shared foundation helps us build the relationships.
- Focusing on giving first. This usually starts with asking, "How can I help you?" This approach, along with other strategies and tactics, has brought us both successful careers and fulfilling professional and personal friendships.
- Being passionate about helping people grow in their careers and businesses by managing the nuances of building their networks.

Questions about networking

The following are some of the most common questions that people ask us about networking:

- What is a network?
- Why do I hate networking?
- Can I change my attitude?
- Isn't this mostly a big time waster?
- What is my philosophy as to how I should network?
- Who should I bring into my network?
- Where should I network?
- What types of organizations or associations should I join?
- How can I network most effectively?
- How big should I grow my network?
- How can I network well while keeping my values?
- What types of people are the best networking partners?
- I don't know a lot of powerful people or have big-name connections—does that matter?
- Won't giving away my connections hurt my business?

Which of the above questions resonate with you? If there are many of the above questions that you wonder about, you're not alone. Networking, especially in a world centered around social media, can be very confusing.

Throughout this book we'll share our experiences and thoughts about the above questions. For example, in response to the first one, *what is a network,* the answer is that each of us has many networks. We walk in and out of our different networks every day. Understanding the many networks in your daily life is the first step in your journey to optimize your networking.

We all network differently, so don't worry if your comfort level is higher or lower than someone else's. It takes practice. Making your net *work* doesn't happen overnight, and there is no silver bullet. We'll help you develop a strategy and a set of tactics that will work best for you. As with any skill set, knowing your goals and personality, your social style, and your current strengths, is critical.

Networking effectively changed our perceptions of ourselves and our career paths, but most of all, it changed our lives for the better. We would never have met the people we talk about in this book had we not made a commitment to strategic networking as a way of growing our careers, and improving our lives and the lives of so many others.

You can't get there from here

Many people see networking as little more than swapping business cards and idle chitchat. That's why this book is so important. We both realized that we need to help people, especially young people starting off in their careers, understand that knowing and then practicing strategic networking can make all the difference.

Again, we see the need to understand both the art and science of career and business networking. The connection between art and science was fine-tuned hundreds of years ago during the Renaissance that began in Florence, Italy, in the fourteenth century. The word *renaissance* means *rebirth*. Melissa believes that today's content-driven, creative world is actually undergoing a second Renaissance, just as Lorenzo de' Medici ushered in an age of prosperity and wealth. This was driven by art but also coupled with a passion to explore the power of human innovation through science.

Melissa and I also believe, as did the Medici and many others during the Renaissance, that at the intersection of art and science is the *divine*—something bigger than ourselves that emerges when we combine both a creative approach (art) and a proven process approach (science). We then use these blended insights to help you build career or business networks that are vibrant and sustainable. Melissa would call the impact of networking this way *possibility expansive*. As Albert Einstein once said, "All religions, arts, and sciences are branches of the same tree. All these aspirations are directed toward ennobling man's life, lifting it from the sphere of mere physical existence and leading the individual towards freedom." We couldn't say it any better.

A relational vs. transactional approach

A lot of people look at business development from a transactional side, an approach usually associated with numbers. For example, if you were in my industry of executive search – which places senior executives into the C-suites of major companies around the world – and you wanted to get two new searches a month, you might have to make thirty connections. Maybe half of those lead to meetings (so that's fifteen meetings) and, of those meetings, maybe two or three turn into searches.

Juxtapose the above scenario against another approach. My scenario may take longer in terms of development, but you'll have an opportunity for an even larger impact and the opportunity for deeper connections. This means building your network *relationally*, where you focus first on what you can do for others versus *transactionally*, where you focus first on what you can do for yourself

Many people take a transactional approach as they implement a very traditional form of networking. Here, your goal may be to just get a referral or, at the very least, an introduction to new connections who could lead to new business or a job opportunity. But, often, this approach actually limits your opportunities because those with whom you network end up feeling as if they've been used rather than helped.

In contrast, a relational approach is more strategic and enlightened. Here, you recognize that those you connect with are *networking partners*. As partners, you both have many more possibilities to exchange opportunities over and over again. Further, you'll find that that your opportunities will expand because you stayed connected, building better, deeper, more significant relationships.

Social scientists and social psychologists often reference the science of influence and persuasion with a focus on what is termed the Rule of Reciprocity. This is a social rule that states that people will give you back something equal to or greater than what you give them. Robert Cialdini, bestselling author of books on influence and persuasion, emphasizes that the Rule of Reciprocity exists in all cultures. Throughout this book, we will show you how taking this rule and applying it to your networking initiatives will help you achieve success in your business or career faster and better.

You *can* get there from *here*

You might be thinking that you have to start by nurturing and maintaining connections with thousands of people. This belief has developed primarily as a result of the online social media boom. However, contrary to this approach to growing your network, you can become very successful by building a small group of well-chosen relationships. In fact, this is the most effective way to achieve your goals. Robin Dunbar was the first researcher to point out that none of us can sustain meaningful relationships with much more than 150 people at any one time. His discovery is referred to as Dunbar's number.[1] Building on his findings, it's much more effective to

---

1 Maria Konnikova, "The Limits of Friendship," *New Yorker*, October 7, 2014, http://www.newyorker.com/science/maria-konnikova/social-media-affect-math-dunbar-number-friendships

start by building ongoing exchanges with a much smaller, high-quality network.

What we've learned is that networking as most people define it today, is rarely effective. You can have twenty-five thousand names in your online database, but the most meaningful, sustainable connections, most of the time, are those in your 150-person circle.

The levels of effective networking

The diagram below shares the various levels you can attain when you network strategically using our focus on building relationally rather than transactionally. Here are explanations of each level:

LEVEL 1: Traditional networking

This is, more often than not, haphazard and random. You're lucky if you get a few results from all those "social gatherings."

LEVEL 2: Strategic networking

Now you're on the right path. You focus on quality connections for the longer term with a goal of helping first. From here you build sustainable relationships with networking partners with whom you regularly *exchange* opportunities.

LEVEL 3: Mentoring, strategic alliances, partnering

You consistently grow your networking partnerships into lifelong professional friendships of mutual support. These are people who not only help you realize your goals but they are also part of *how* you reach your goals. Along the way they offer lots of wisdom along with introductions and referrals to new people and opportunities.

LEVEL 4: Sponsorships

Here you *champion* one another into greater positions of influence. This involves promoting each other throughout the process of getting new business or career opportunities.

LEVEL 5: Connection hubs

Now you've hit your stride. You are creating *connection hubs,* powerful networks that yield continuous new opportunities for everyone involved. These might include clubs, networking groups, and committees that you create and lead.

HIERARCHY OF NETWORKING

Level 5 — CONNECTION HUBS

Level 4 — SPONSORSHIPS

Level 3 — MENTORING/STRATEGIC ALLIANCES/PARTNERING

Level 2 — STRATEGIC NETWORKING

Level 1 — TRADITIONAL NETWORKING

Exploring networking further

In his bestselling book *The Tipping Point*, social scientist Malcolm Gladwell identifies *the Law of the Few*, which states that "a very small number of people are linked to everyone else in a few steps (or human connections), and the rest of us are linked to the world through those special few."[2] The advent of social media and people growing enormous networks online has certainly altered the size of these networks, but we believe the research is still valid.

Gladwell further points out that very few people are great networkers. We add that, again, it's those smaller groups and one-to-one networking partnerships that will make your net *work* more effectively than accumulating thousands of online friends.

Every day we miss out on creating the optimum conditions for networking. We're not building significant, sustainable one-to-one and small-group relationships. Think about it. How many times do you see a group of people sitting together at a restaurant, all of them on their respective cell phones, posting out to their friends on Facebook? We'll help you see the paradox of slowing down to speed up the creation of networking partnerships that will benefit you and your partners much more effectively.

Beginning with my college study tutor, and followed by so many others over the years, I learned that, more than anything, networking is about relationships where all parties connect, support, and care about one another. You have one another's back.

---

2 Malcolm Gladwell, *The Tipping Point: How Little Things Can Make a Big Difference* (Boston: Back Bay Books, 2002).

The networking knowledge gap

Looking back at the diagram on the five levels of networking, we emphasize again that most people are stuck at the first level and even if they do move up to any of the other levels, they will, most likely, do so unconsciously and haphazardly much like I did until I started studying the processes other top networkers, like Melissa, had created, tested and continuously improved over the years.

But through the last two years of us researching the current state of business networking, we discovered that there still exists a very real "networking knowledge gap." We can see strong evidence of this gap in the disparity between mentoring programs and business networking programs in schools, companies and other organizations. We found that there are more than ten times the number of mentoring programs than networking programs in existence and there doesn't appear to be strong efforts to close this gap . . . yet.

So what can be done? We suggest that organizations and schools of all sizes start to implement formal business networking programs. These programs will dramatically improve the levels of success of everyone involved while also significantly improving the job search market and the general economic prosperity of our communities as more people exchange ongoing business opportunities with one another.

In the meantime, throughout this book we will share our best practices with you to help you network more successfully to help you quickly close any knowledge gaps when it comes to your networking.

We believe the biggest problem with networking is that what we know about the subject hasn't been integrated into our learning institutions or business environments. This knowledge gap exists all over the world. Neither schools nor businesses have given networking the attention and development it requires to help others grow their careers. Study after study shows that networking accounts for as much as 70 percent of how jobs are acquired, kept, and changed—so why wouldn't anyone who wants a successful career need to learn more about developing their networking skills?[3]

This glaring disparity between the statistical evidence of networking's effectiveness and the lack of formal business networking programs in schools and corporations is nothing short of perplexing.

How do you feel about networking?

What happens when you go to a networking event or your manager tells you that you need to network? Do your palms sweat? Does your heart start racing? Or do you actually get excited?

If you're like most people, you have a negative reaction. We haven't done scientific studies on the question of what percentage of people dislike networking, but we think it's safe to say it's a lot. Plenty of people really hate the process. Many of these people have either been

---

[3] Bob McIntosh, "80% of Today's Jobs Are Landed through Networking," *Recruiting Blogs*, March 26, 2012, http://www.recruitingblogs.com/profiles/blogs/80-of-today-s-jobs-are-landed-through-networking;
Susan Adams, "Networking Is Still the Best Way to Find a Job, Survey Says," *Forbes*, June 7, 2011, http://www.forbes.com/sites/susanadams/2011/06/07/networking-is-still-the-best-way-to-find-a-job-survey-says/#2a2d800c2754.

told they need to network, or they see others doing it or talking about it. So they just go out with their goal being to meet as many people as possible, and they do so without developing a connection.

But to really gain an insight into why so many dislike networking, let's look further into research we have discovered that addresses these reasons.

CHAPTER 3

Ten Reasons Why People Dislike Networking

Because networking is a key ingredient for career and business success, it's the people who have trouble with it who often find themselves held back in their careers. Therefore, it's beneficial to identify the reasons for disliking the process. From there we can address necessary adjustments to overcome those hurdles.

If you have negative feelings about networking, the list, below, may help you uncover what may be holding you back. Perhaps you can relate to one or more of them. This could also benefit someone you know who needs to overcome their fear and network more effectively to improve their professional life.

1. Feeling awkward

Meeting people for the first time can be an uncomfortable experience, even for those extroverts and social butterflies among us. The whole idea of not knowing anything about the person you're talking to makes many people feel extremely awkward. Some people find being around strangers so unsettling that they either make absolutely no effort to get to know them, or they remain too timid to pursue a relationship and take advantage of possible opportunities. Feelings of awkwardness are compounded when networking activities take place in unfamiliar locations with large numbers of unknown people milling about.

Awkwardness toward networking generally has its roots in shyness that causes varying degrees of anxiety. A survey conducted by *Psychology Today* revealed that 62 percent of participants experienced shyness on a daily basis, while 82 percent considered the feeling to be "undesirable."[4] Respondents were from various ethnic backgrounds and education levels, revealing the scope of the problem.

Most people are affected by natural shyness that can be overcome with some effort and by using various strategies. However, some people are plagued by a form of shyness that is categorized as a social phobia; it affects mood and behavior and often requires the assistance of psychologists and prescribed medications to be overcome. A 2011 study found that only 12 percent of those who identified themselves as shy actually met the clinical criteria for the phobia.[5] If you consider yourself to be shy, you probably don't need to worry. Natural shyness can be overcome by improving confidence and self-esteem. One

---

4   Bernardo Carducci and Philip G. Zimbardo, "The Cost of Shyness," *Psychology Today,* November 1, 1995, https://www.psychologytoday.com/articles/199511/the-cost-shyness.

5   Marcy Burstein, Leila Ameli-Grillon, and Kathleen R. Merikangas, "Shyness Versus Social Phobia in US Youth," Pediatrics, October 2011, doi: 10.1542/peds.2011-1434.

of the best ways to do that is to practice making conversation with people with whom you're already familiar. You can also turn to social media you do like, such as Facebook or Twitter.

2. Not knowing who to approach

Many people who are willing to try networking are hampered by not knowing which people to approach. The average person passes by or comes in contact with dozens of people throughout the day, any number of whom could potentially be beneficial contacts. The sheer volume of possible contacts can make deciding which individuals are the best prospects a daunting endeavor. Even when provided with more specific information, such as identifying a particular company to visit, it can be confusing, embarrassing, and intimidating simply because you may know the company, but not know the best person to talk to.

The good news is, when networking, anyone can be the "right one" who provides that certain opportunity or assistance that is advantageous to your goal. The secret is finding people with whom you connect with naturally. That's why it's important to practice networking consistently at every available opportunity. However, you can significantly improve your odds of finding the "jewels" by focusing on, first, just one person with whom you feel a natural connection. From there find out one person that connection admires and believes is a good connection. It's better to go slowly and develop one great connection at a time than to rush the process.

3. Not knowing what to say

A lot of people dislike networking because they're at a loss for words when they meet someone. Those who actually put forth the effort to attend events and meet people oftentimes have their momentum stopped abruptly by not knowing what to say once the initial introduction has occurred. Whether or not you've experienced such a moment, not knowing what to say when you meet a stranger can kill an otherwise great opportunity to open up a new relationship.

Many people may also be at a loss for words because they believe they need to begin with business talk when they first start to network. However, starting with a social connection where you recognize something more personal about an individual—such as a story they told that illuminated a passion they have, or even something as simple as complimenting them on their suit—can begin to build a business friendship.

There are also people who consider networking to be all about small talk. Through our research, we have found that many people look at networking as talking about things like the weather or, even simpler, questions about the quality of your current day. But as we'll show you, searching for common connections takes your small talk to a deeper level.

Networking is more effective when you're able to find not one, but multiple connections with someone. Maybe you grew up in the same town or had the same major in college. By digging deeper around our common connections (Melissa and I discovered we both had worked at Cedar Point Amusement Park in Sandusky, Ohio, around the same time), we find other ones we didn't realize we had.

We'll share more about moving beyond small talk later, but for now, realize that most of us are prisoners of small talk and, as such, we're not taking full advantage of all that a more significant conversation around connections can create.

4. Fearing rejection

People possess an instinctive desire to be accepted and the possibility of being rejected, demeaned, or isolated produces insecurities that can often cripple one's ability to proceed with productive activities.[6]

Those who fear rejection, yet are pressured to network, tend to stumble in their efforts because they turn to people they already know or are comfortable with to make their pitches. Even more aggressive networkers who suffer from this fear may thwart opportunities by cutting off relationships prematurely in an effort to avoid preconceived hurts before they occur. If fear of rejection is hurting your efforts, it helps to realize that the person you're talking with may well be feeling the same thing.

---

6 John Amodeo, "Deconstructing the Fear of Rejection," *Psychology Today,* April 4, 2014. https://www.psychologytoday.com/blog/intimacy-path-toward-spirituality/201404/deconstructing-the-fear-rejection.

5. Feeling pressured

It's true that networking is heavily influenced by the desire of everyone involved to gain something advantageous. Whether you're seeking a job lead, a new sales contact, a location to expand to, or any other target, it involves telling people what you want. This can make you feel vulnerable. Although some people are more refined in their networking approach, others can be aggressive. Many are put off by such behavior. They may feel that certain expectations are placed on them, whether real or imagined.

The business world tends to compound such pressures by constantly demanding more from those within its grasp. Well-meaning loved ones, teammates, and other armchair counselors may tell you that pressure makes you perform better. However, according to psychologists Hendrie Weisinger and J. P. Pawliw-Fry, pressure more commonly diminishes the effects of performance and often leads to utter failure.[7] It's far better to learn how to minimize pressure from all fronts, including the pressure you put on yourself, so you can be free to realize better success with networking.

6. Feeling like a pest

While some networkers feel pressure to be aggressive, others wrestle with the fear that their networking will be interpreted as annoying. These people believe they're pestering people, particularly when their goals are based on developing a constant stream of inquiries, data

---

[7] Hendrie Weisinger and J. P. Pawliw-Fry, *Performing Under Pressure: The Science of Doing Your Best When It Matters Most*. New York: Crown Business, 2015.

mining, and sales pitches. They can feel as though they're coming across as desperate to make a sale. This can lead to significantly toning down networking efforts or avoiding making contacts altogether.

7. Having trouble keeping track of contacts

Another chore created by networking is keeping up with contacts. Relationships grow by regularly reaching out to and conversing with people. Since the core of networking is to make relationships that can be beneficial at some point in time, effort has to be made to reconnect with important contacts. This can be trying for someone who lacks organizational skills, finds it difficult to talk to acquaintances, or has high demands on their time.

The following up with contacts is an essential part of the networking process. This is reflected in a CareerXroads survey that shows that 65 percent of all job openings are filled through the referrals of others.[8] Another study from the same source revealed that nearly 27 percent of hires come from external sources, many of which are gathered through networking efforts.[9] In this age of technologically-advanced communication tools, following up with valuable networking contacts is both easy and convenient. So why do people still find it difficult to follow up? The reasons are varied, from not having

---

8   Gerry Crispin and Mark Mehler, 10th Annual CareerXroads Source of Hire Report: By the Numbers, March 2011, http://www.careerxroads.com/news/SourcesOfHire11.pdf.

9   Gerry Crispin and Mark Mehler, 9th Annual CareerXroads Source of Hire Study: Meltdown in 2009 and What It Means for a 2010 Recovery, February 2010, http://www.careerxroads.com/news/SourcesOfHire10.pdf.

enough time to lacking the skills or know-how. It's mostly an issue of self-discipline: deciding to do it and then following through.

8. Not always feeling up to it

The core task that underlies all aspects of networking is maintaining a positive attitude with every contact during every encounter. However, most people find it difficult to maintain a consistent, positive mood at all times. A variety of life issues can arise, leaving you feeling glum or even depressed, and putting on a smile and conjuring up a chipper attitude can be challenging or even impossible. When people feel down, they tend to seek refuge in safe places away from threats. These threats may include the presence of new and different people. And, because making new contacts usually requires a happy disposition to produce positive results, trying to network when you feel miserable is not only extremely taxing, but also unproductive.

Luckily, there are a number of strategies to achieve success in networking even when you feel down in the dumps. For example, you can ensure you get sufficient rest and breaks to recharge your battery; eat right so your health is at its peak; attend smaller, less stressful networking events; and set goals that are less demanding during down times.

9. Believing that networking is a waste of time

We fill up our schedules with countless activities, all demanding to be done immediately. Work, errands, meetings, outings with family and friends, and other responsibilities can make pressing demands on our time. Many people consider networking to be a waste of time because they feel they could be engaging in higher-priority activities, or that their time spent networking doesn't produce satisfactory results.

Richard Stromback, a successful entrepreneur, venture capitalist, and former professional hockey player, agrees that a great deal of networking is a waste of time. Concerning the annual mega-networking conference dubbed Davos (because of its location in Davos, Switzerland), which is attended by the world's elite, Stromback suggests, "The answer is to be extremely efficient and focus on what is truly essential."[10] If this can be said about the largest networking event in the world, then it also holds true for any networking endeavor.

10. Feeling dirty

The last, but definitely not least, reason why people dislike networking is that they're made to feel unclean by participating in networking events—especially when they're expected to attend. This idea is backed up by a recent study that utilized a series of experiments to gauge how people consciously and subconsciously feel about the process.[11]

---

10   Greg McKeown, "99% of Networking Is a Waste of Time," *Harvard Business Review,* January 22, 2015, https://hbr.org/2015/01/99-of-networking-is-a-waste-of-time.

11   Tiziana Casciaro, Francesca Gino, and Maryam Kouchaki, "The Contaminating Effects of Building Instrumental Ties: How Networking Can Make Us Feel Dirty," April 28, 2014, Harvard Business School NOM Unit Working Paper No. 14-108, doi: 10.2139/ssrn.2430174.

A majority of study participants involved in planned networking events were more likely to have negative feelings here than when they networked with others under more natural conditions.

Melissa and I have both hosted many networking events. We have also both attended many events. What we would offer here is that our events are both a combination of structure and natural networking with our emphasis on *facilitating* connections—what we believe to be the key differentiator between effective and ineffective networking.

When it comes down to it, networking is something that everyone has participated in on various levels throughout their life. We've met and built relationships with new teachers, neighbors, friends, coworkers, and so on, and we've utilized those relationships to find jobs, exchange news or opportunities, and refer others to friends or vendors we know. In a nutshell, that's what networking boils down to.

The key difference with business or career networking is that here you have more specific goals, usually to gain some particular benefit or advantage, but you can't achieve your goals as effectively until you realize how to create networks that work over time. The best first step you can take is to, first, look at networking as a process *of opening up a relationship with someone* Meeting the right networking partners and investing in them will bring you closer to fulfilling your goals and desires more than any other career or business growth success strategy we know.

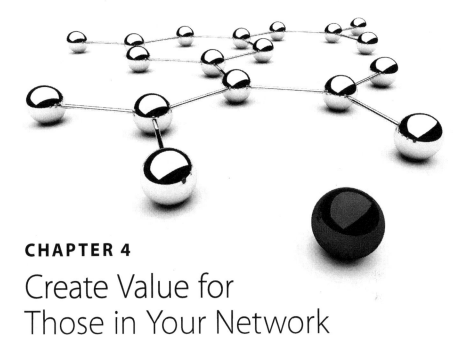

CHAPTER 4

Create Value for Those in Your Network

The foundation for building a net that *works* starts with creating value for those in your network. Here, begin with the question, "How can I help?" This enables, first, a *connection*, and then a *direction* to your conversation.

It's about making a plan for your life that helps others get where they want to be. We embrace what leading motivational speaker Zig Ziglar once said, "You can get everything in life you want, if you will just help enough other people get what they want."

It's never too late to become an effective networker. Whether you realize it or not, you've been making friends and connections your entire life, Now you just need to learn how to enhance those connections. If you read this entire book and implement even a few of our tips and strategies, you'll definitely experience better results.

Additionally, if you're persistent in your new practices, you'll see a continuous stream of results over time.

We're sure you've met people who come at networking purely systematically, not from the heart or with the intention to help others. If you're one of these people, we want you to know that there's a part of this that you'll be very good at—the *science* of creating networks. But to be truly successful, you have to learn the *art* that includes the emotional elements of networking and the creativity that helps you see possibilities in relationships that others who take a strictly logical approach can miss.

Take, for example, a situation Melissa experienced when she was waiting to meet members of an audience she had just spoken to after keynoting for their annual conference. One of the stories she had shared during her keynote involved her co-author on her *Networlding* book. After shaking hands with about ten people who were waiting in line to speak with her, a man walked up, greeting her with the statement, "Just tell me how to get in touch with your co-author. I want to do business with her company."

Not missing a beat, Melissa thanked the man for coming and stated firmly, "I'm sorry. That's not the way I network. If you had listened to my talk, you'd know that approaching people in the way you approached me will not help you get what you want."

The man just looked at her and asked two more times for an introduction. She added that the way to connect effectively is to, first, be genuine, look for values you have in common (my focus on making a connection), and then work toward helping one another. This is when making introductions can be made. Again, Melissa stated that was not the way to network effectively. Eventually, the man left, after she kept responding, kindly but firmly, that he was not behaving in a manner that would benefit his chances of getting an introduction.

What does this story show us? Networking takes tact and creativity, what I would term the *art* side. But it also takes strategy, the *science* side, to create value for both parties to continue building connection and support for one another. A better strategy would have been for the man to first share something that he found useful from the talk Melissa gave. Now, he would have to work hard to re-open a door to even talk with Melissa again.

We get it that many people don't understand this starting path to add value to your network. For example, there's someone I work with, a wonderfully talented woman with an MBA from a top university. We'll call her Carla. Carla *loathes* the idea of networking. Just the thought of going to events, pressing palms all night, gathering up stacks of business cards, and so on, gives her shivers and mild panic attacks. She says, "Billy, that's work for me. I have to work at networking. I only do this because it makes sense to connect with colleagues and clients."

Carla is not alone in her dread. So, I responded to Carla's complaints. "I have to work at it, too. But because I'm aware that so many people have problems with it, over time I developed, a process that helps me move past any issues I may have with networking to focus instead on how I can help others." This is all about starting to add value to that person by building a connection. It's about *giving first*.

I explained that there are three basic but important steps in my networking process, each with its own set of practices, each important and even essential to success:

- My first step is to find common ground, values, and interests between me and the person I'm networking with. This step lays the groundwork for the next two steps.

- My second step involves asking questions like, "What do you currently need?" and "How can I be helpful to you?"

- My third step is where I ask the important question of myself, "How can I connect this person to someone valuable in my network?"

I'm very aware of the time this takes. The amount of time it takes to network effectively is often why many people complain that networking isn't worth the effort. But these people fail to see that time is their investment in their success and, also, in the success of their networking partners. These same people won't hesitate to work to make money to buy whatever they need to achieve success, yet they don't see how building a vibrant network can dramatically accelerate their career goals.

I've found that my investment in building a powerful network has yielded sustainable success for me and for my networking partners. There's no question that successful networking takes persistence and perseverance. But having faith is about giving with no expectations. Then, couple that attitude with the confidence that you're traveling along on the right path, that you have the right set of intentions. This is the *art* part. It connects to your heart. If you're authentic, you're already on the way there when it comes to adding value to networking.

When I was just starting my career I had to figure this out personally, professionally, socially, and spiritually. I relocated to Chicago in 1990 and didn't know anyone. I had no other choice. I couldn't go back home. I needed to move forward in my life. My belief in God actually ended up bringing me opportunities beyond anything I dreamed about. That was seven companies and eight homes ago, which includes several years in New York.

I remember working at Motorola, helping them with recruiting. Because I was working with engineers, it wasn't until I used one of their own tools (an engineering process map) to point out the cycle time and beyond of the recruiting process, that they really got what I was saying. I was speaking their language, referencing milestones and quarterly and annual goals. This made recruiting relevant to them and, from there, I was able to build strong networks of trust and support.

I made a connection with them by taking the time to understand *their* language which was my way of connecting with them. This is where you too can start to build effective networks. Effective networking starts with taking the time to build the social glue to create connections. Make significant, mutually beneficial connections today, and, even more importantly, on a continuous basis, and you'll start to see results that keep on creating benefits to your whole network. I call this building social capital/making an investment in building your network. You must always invest in the future with your relationships. This is the concept of building your net before you need it. Then if you take a fall, you've got your net. That's how your *net works* best.

This practice goes beyond business to more of an emotional connection. Your network becomes your lifeline at times. Those in your network don't *owe* you anything, but you'll find, if you build the right network, those in it are there for you in friendship, reaching out and going the extra mile for you when you ask for help. Start by creating significant relationships with a social-friendship foundation prior to initiating a business relationship. You want your connections to lead to relationships that thrive and sustain you through the usual ups and downs of life. It's all about initiating value-based relationships.

Initiating value-based relationships by telling your story

At a recent business networking event at a restaurant, I said to a group I was talking with, "Why don't we go around the table and share our stories?" I developed this strategy partially because of something my good friend Steve Pemberton, Chief Diversity Officer at Walgreens, says in his great book, *A Chance in the World*, "We don't look like our stories." In this case, there was a very polished woman in the group who, to our surprise, shared, "I was a refugee." We were stunned. She looked nothing like a refugee. This created a great amount of interest and curiosity about her life.

She told us the story of how she and her family first came to the US to escape poverty in her country and they had lived in a refugee camp. This experience got me thinking how it's the deeper conversations that can create the bigger or even biggest opportunities in our lives. What happened from this woman opening up to her authentic story was the sharing of her struggles, unknown to us, real to her, was enlightening for all. From her story, we all started sharing more deeply about our respective struggles along the way to success. This experience that day helped all of us heal a bit from our own challenges, while simultaneously creating a deeper bond among all of at the table. When it came to my turn, I shared a memory that still impacts my life today.

It was the early 1980s. I was a sophomore at Saginaw Valley State University. Christmas was only a short time away and I found myself really strapped for cash. So when Christmas break came and I landed a job in the men's department at J.C. Penney in the local mall, I was really excited about the opportunity to make some extra money. The store was about a mile from campus, and although I could walk there, one of my friends lent me her car so I could come and go more easily through the deep snow.

It was the first week of December and exams were over. I decided to stay until Christmas Eve. Days before everyone left, my friends kept asking with wide eyes, "Are you really planning to stay here on your own?" I didn't understand what the fuss was about. I didn't think it was such a big deal that I would be all alone. When I asked the resident hall director, Carol, if I could stay from Christmas through New Year's, she gave me the green light. But I could see her eyes saying something quite different like, "Gee, Billy. You aren't going to spend time with your family? I feel for you and wish you had other options."

Everyone had left the campus for Christmas break, except me. I was OK the first couple of days after everyone left. It was actually kind of fun having the whole campus to myself, listening to my favorite music, making mix tapes, and sleeping in late. But after about three days, my ghost-town campus grew eerie and echoed with emptiness. I yearned for the company of my friends and family members. I missed my mom and my brother, with whom I'd spent the last nineteen years celebrating those special family days before Christmas. I kept telling myself that it would be worth it, once I got paid. So I plodded on, pushing myself to keep a cheery face and constant smile while ringing up one clothing gift after another.

The days went by slowly, but finally, it was just one day before Christmas. I was going home! But then I turned on the news and my heart lurched. There was a huge storm coming my way. I had to make a decision. Should I take a chance and risk getting stuck on the road in the snow in the middle of a blizzard? Or should I stay and miss Christmas with my mom and brother for the first time ever?

I wrestled with my options. Eventually I decided to stay. I reasoned that the day after Christmas would be an even bigger shopping day than the days before it. I really needed the money for Christmas presents and, even more importantly, to pay for expenses for my next semester.

My decision resulted in the loneliest Christmas I ever had. I spent that Christmas mixing Prince's greatest hits and party jams on my cassette tapes. I took all my albums and 45s and put these mixes together. And, believe it or not, I still have those cassettes!

After I was able to make it through Christmas, I decided to stay on campus until school started again. I busied myself, working during the day, making sure I clocked as many hours as possible so I would be exhausted and just sleep when I returned back to my dorm each evening on the empty campus.

Finally, it was time for school to start again. Everyone came back from their vacations sharing happy memories. I decided to keep my secret to myself. No one from school knew that I had stayed on campus the entire time, and I didn't tell anyone. I just couldn't. I was too embarrassed and I didn't want anyone to feel sorry for me.

Yet, I did learn something from that lonely time. That experience taught me that I could get along in the world by myself. However, I also learned that I deeply needed and wanted the friendship of others in my life, whether I was working or socializing. That's why, since that lonely Christmas break in college, one of my top priorities has been to build networks of supportive colleagues.

When I returned to my classes, I started back with more eagerness around developing my network than ever before. Of course, I also paid attention to my schoolwork. I was dedicated to making sure I would have the kind of life that combined business with social, an important mix because I had seen, even back then, that the social sides of our lives dramatically impact our business lives.

I was so grateful to have the opportunity college offered me. I will be eternally grateful to those first people who helped me get into college. Those early mentors helped me build the belief that I could do anything with my life. I could go anywhere. This belief in myself helped me move beyond my humble beginnings. Education was certainly my ticket to a better life, to break the cycle of not having any career direction.

For many, graduating from college is considered a rite of passage. For me, it was an honor. Since Saginaw Valley State University, I've had to reinvent myself many times—so often, in fact, that I eventually became unafraid to start over, again and again and take risks. But it was that first leg of my adult journey at Saginaw Valley that gave me the many lessons that have sustained me well throughout my life.

Saginaw Valley was truly the start of my journey down the networking path. I was part of my parents' story until then. But then going away to college allowed me to create my own story. It was then that I took a turn in my road. I chose a different path that no one in my family had ever traveled. I also chose to keep marching down that new path. I made that path my own and I kept going. I remember the words of Dr. Robert Schuller, the Christian evangelist and host of the show Hour of Power, which I often watched on TV. He once said, as if he was speaking only to me, "If it's going to be, it's up to me." Those words march through my mind even now. They have influenced my life path and are the foundation of how I make my net *work*.

Dr. Schuller's words were also responsible for leading me to Melissa. I had the honor of being chosen by her and her team as one of the top networkers in the world for a contest she ran back in 2002. Then in 2007, after writing seven books, she took her passion for writing to the next level and started giving back to other thought leaders who wanted to author books by conducting writers' workshops. That's when Melissa and I reconnected and bonded, and when I decided to start working on a book of my own.

But it wasn't until seven years later that Melissa and I were meeting to talk about my book that I finally figured out *how* I was going to tell my story. You see, although I went to Melissa's workshop back in 2007 and I did engage Melissa to help me write my book, I didn't start my book officially until a cold November afternoon in 2014. It was a divine moment.

But it still took decades later for me to start really sharing my story out to the world. That happened in 2014 when Melissa and I met for our usual annual get together. This year she brought with her a beautiful Levenger leather journal to give me with my name embossed on the cover. It was a gift to me for referring quite a few of my colleagues and friends to her would had shared with me they too wanted to write books.

I remember patiently listening to Melissa thank me for the referrals I had given to her over the years. Then I paused and said, "Melissa, please listen to me and don't say anything until I am through."

She immediately saw I had changed my tone and, sitting up even straighter than she was already, replied, "OK. Go ahead." I proceeded to tell her that I absolutely knew the path I should now take. I looked her in the eyes and said, "I want to write the book with you."

She paused, took a deep breath, and said quietly but firmly, "OK. Let's do that."

Once again, I felt a sense of deep gratitude. I was hoping that, like me, Melissa was at that point in her life path that she knew herself well enough that when an opportunity arose, she would seize it and not look back. I was glad to see she was right there with me. Now, we just had to sit down and really work to bring our two very different paths together to create the kind of value we could only create by letting go and letting something bigger than ourselves emerge.

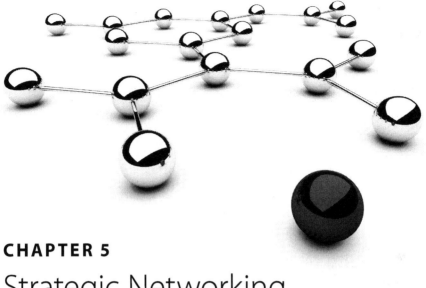

CHAPTER 5
Strategic Networking

I've been fine-tuning my approach to networking for over twenty-five years, but even at a young age I valued making connections and creating sustainable relationships. It wasn't until later in life, after becoming a professional, that I truly understood the value of networking in creating relationship currency—the result of developing relationships and connections that matter.

Indeed, other people recognized my ability to network before I did. I would constantly hear people say, "Wow, Billy, you know everyone, or everyone knows you!" Only after many years did I realize that I was networking strategically and consistently. But I was into my thirties before I read George Fraser's book, *Success Runs in Our Race: The Complete Guide to Effective Networking*. It was then that I realized I was creating a process that made my networking more of a science.

I discovered this after doing some research around networking, and this realization helped me create even stronger relationships. To this end I developed connections with many people and expanded my network, but my networking didn't end there. Effective networking meant *staying in touch* with my connections and also *introducing people to others* to further their success.

Then, because I had a passion for giving back, I also wanted to share what I had learned through practicing and building my networking skills. At this time, 1996, I worked for Motorola, traveling around the country, recruiting at the top twenty-five universities. I found myself constantly being asked to come back and present my insights on networking for college students. Over time I became aware that maybe God had blessed me with the gift of networking excellence. I felt compelled to share what I had learned with as many people as possible. This is the reason why I became a *networking evangelist and a connector.* I understood the power having a strong network could create, and wanted to help others build their own networks.

Shortly after this awakening, I further realized that networking and relationships were not only *currency,* but also that networking is one of the top skills one needs to be successful in a career or business. Further, the relationships you build add up to define how people view you. If they view you as a value-added resource, people will refer business to you. If they don't, you will find you don't get referrals or don't get as many referrals as you could be getting.

Start by building a wise networking philosophy. Don't make building your network just about creating a safety net in case you lose your job, or a circle of connections who will help you get meetings to sell your products or services, or to have someone open doors that will allow you to rub elbows with leaders in your industry. Your network is so much more than that, and as such, your philosophy should be something deeper and focused on how you can, first, help others. Again, the science of networks validates that the rule of reciprocity works when the parties involved have no hidden agenda when they offer support to someone else. The reason is that when you have ulterior motives not only will others see through your support, but also, you lose the focus that is needed to truly benefit others. This focus is about you being authentic and transparent.

Strategic networking starts with building a values-based personal brand

At Heidrick, first, we're hired because of our strong brand, our capabilities and our track record of success. Heidrick has been in this business for over sixty years. Second, we're hired because of our individual brands and our ability to connect to leadership talent. We're hired to connect and recruit a specific type of person. Let's say there are ten people who might be suited for a certain position, all of whom are well-qualified. Our job is to find the person who fits the *culture and has the skill sets and professional experience needed* of the organization that has hired us. In order to do this we have to really know each person. This *connection process* is the foundation of what I do. My goal is to put people in positions where they can play to their *strengths*—where they can be most successful.

So what is your personal brand? Start by taking an inventory by answering the following questions:

- What are you known for at work? Is it your ability to listen well or perhaps you are the person who plans all the outings for your team or maybe you are the connector who is constantly introducing the new people to those seasoned in your organization.

- What are you known for among your friends? Might it be your clever stories or your fun-loving attitude about life? Or could it be your constant thoughtfulness?

Trust and strategic networking

Bob Burg, bestselling author of *The Go-Giver* and *Adversaries into Allies,* sums up what it means to have a network fueled by trust: He states, "By a network, I don't necessarily mean your customers or clients. I mean a network of people who know you, like you, and trust you. They might never buy anything from you, but they've always got you in the backs of their minds. They're people who are personally invested in seeing you succeed… They're your army of personal walking ambassadors."

What Burg is describing is what happens when you thoughtfully and strategically create networks of ongoing support. These relationships are based on building trust over time. They are also the networks where you can create what Melissa terms, *transference of trust*. This is the outcome of people either introducing you or referring you to others in their networks that you have yet to meet. The power of *transference of trust* makes for ongoing growth of the networks of all parties involved.

As Melissa and I both built our careers, we discovered a secret: if you're good at building relationships, opportunities will present themselves. The best way to get a job or get a new client or customer is to know someone who knows someone, or even better, to know someone who knows many "someones."

But challenges arise when you meet people who only want to meet those who can do something *for them*. This leads to an imbalance where more people are trying to help *themselves* versus helping others.

This notion was backed up when Melissa assigned three interns to find out whether people had more *givers* or more *takers* in their networks. The interns trekked through the streets of downtown Chicago during one of its busy, summer lunch hours. They shoved their camcorders and microphones into as many faces as possible. In the end, they found most people stated they had more *takers*—people who wanted to take but not give to others when it came to networking. It's hard to believe that people knowingly make this their strategy for networking. This outcome would eventually lead to poor results as people in your network see that they give but never get anything in return. By this we mean even receiving a thank you for what they have received.

Taking, of course, is the wrong way to approach networking. Your focus should be on making connections that are mutually beneficial. But what does that strategic process look like? How does it feel? Think about building a network with intention. Be strategic and deliberate when engaging with your networking partners by considering how to *exchange* opportunities—not just today but for the long term. Melissa has found through interactive networking events, that one of the best questions you can ask to start this process is, "How can we create opportunities for both of us?"

To this end, create a long-term strategy with short-term goals. It's about building a quality versus quantity foundation. This means focusing *not* on the number of people we can get to be in our network, but, instead, those who are *ready, willing* and *able* to connect and exchange support, ideas and opportunities with one another. Don't waste your time on takers. The world is full of them.

Finally, both Melissa and I have fought through many of the negative feelings about networking people have that we addressed earlier in Chapter 3. Eventually, we faced our fears and fought through them. Now we hope you will be able to do the same. It's important to know that you are definitely not alone.

Tips

Following are some more strategies you can put into play as early as tomorrow:

- **Network down as well as up.** Networking down is about being the mentor. Take one colleague of ours, Dave, a president of a large web-design and development company. He acquired a large account because he had befriended and mentored one of their salespeople several years earlier when everyone else would not give this person the time of day. But Dave realized that all people are worth the time it takes to let them know they're important and to provide them with guidance as to how to grow successfully.

- **Treat each person you meet with uncompromising respect.** Great networkers are zealots of respect and integrity. They're like the knights in King Arthur's roundtable. They care about creating relationships of honor.

- **Suspend judgment when you meet someone new.** We often find ourselves meeting people who, upon first glance, don't seem to have the wherewithal to exchange or just don't seem like the sharing type. However, we make it a rule to give each person the opportunity to exchange with us toward the possibility of partnership. We constantly mentor others toward becoming better partners. We see this as a way to teach the world through these people–how to be better at sharing. For instance, Melissa works with a journalist who was formerly homeless. Rather than focus on the "homeless" tag she looked past that, discovered the woman was a TED Global speaker and had connections at the top media outlets in the country. She was also a giver and a networker.

- **Be creative when thinking of people to contact.** Start with people who really like you and brainstorm with them. Get them to give you a few names of people they really like but for one reason or another you have never met.

- **Connect the unconnected.** The research on human networks shows us that the real secret to creating a diverse, continuous and ever-growing flow of new business or career opportunities is to look for people who have yet to be connected. John may be looking for information about Company B and your colleague who works there, Susan, whom John has yet to meet. By linking the two together you create value for John and very likely Susan, who can benefit from knowing someone who may very well become a new team member at her organization.

- **Help people feel wanted.** Recognize that most people want attention. Search for the uniqueness in others. Help them to feel significant. Do this by finding just one or two things about what they have said that you find most beneficial to you. Disclose your thoughts in a blog post or in person, or mention them on Twitter.

At its core, a successful networking process starts with listening. This can be face-to-face, or online. By listening with each of the people we meet when we're networking, we are able to find what matters to them, and from there, help them through our connections. Also our respective ideas for growing our careers or businesses move ahead faster. You can do the same. It's easy. What are your current networking partners interested in? What are their jobs? What do they do in their spare time? What is a fun day for them? Connecting with people is about being honestly interested in what makes them tick.

Find points of commonality

As I shared above, my role involves partnering with companies to help them find executive leadership talent. My goal is to always consider the viewpoint of the person I'm networking with when I search for commonalities between the two of us. I find those commonalities by asking open-ended questions. And to find commonalities, it's important to know yourself well.

Melissa calls these *points of commonality*. In her experience, people often don't probe effectively to discover what they have in common with the people they meet. Here's an example of her doing this with a law firm, asking people to partner up with another person in the firm to explore something they had in common but didn't know about before. Believe it or not, two of the senior partners who had known one another and worked together for twenty-eight years discovered they both played the cello since they were kids and had never realized that.

For years, Melissa facilitated networking sessions with hundreds of people at a time, breaking them up into groups of ten to accelerate the networking process. Her research and results validated the fact that people are more effective when they are able to share more in the smaller rather than larger group experience. She gave participants an exercise she had developed that required them to explore commonalities that were not *self-evident*, such as everyone in the group had eyes or noses, etc. Instead, they had to all have the thing they were probing for around connections, in common, like they all loved to travel or they all loved dogs and so on.

Participants were constantly surprised to discover the many commonalities they would not have otherwise unearthed. Over time Melissa realized that most people talk at a surface level, making what is most often referred to as *small talk*. As a result, they fail to connect in ways that would engage and connect. So they fail to move their relationships to the next level where they can further help one another.

As the years passed, Melissa taught thousands of people how to engage with one another more effectively using a resource she created with Jocelyn Carter Miller, called the Networlding Support Exchange. Here, participants learn how to grow their networks more effectively. This exploration helps them uncover ways they can mutually support one another with both their current and long-term goals. In Chapter 10, "The Science of Making Your Net *Work*," we will share this resource and show you how you can use it effectively.

Another component of making your net *work* is to build self-discipline. Here are the steps:

- **Be in the moment.** Focus totally on the other person and what he or she indicates matters most.

- **Get engaged.** As we mentioned earlier, listening is key to great networking. Engagement starts with listening for understanding. This involves taking the time to figure out what matters most currently to those with whom you network.

- **Prepare questions in advance, especially open-ended ones.** See Chapter 10 for a list of questions that will create engagement on many levels.

- **Create a list of the best questions for generating conversations.** Think of the best questions you can ask to start great conversation and exchanges. For example, "If this were the best year of your life, what would you do?" Or, "What's the best question you've ever been asked?" Ask this question as often as possible of as many people as you can. Soon you'll find great, open-ended questions that unearth *possibilities* that can blossom into opportunities.

- **Keep asking questions.** When *you* do the asking you can lead the conversation toward the most successful outcome and that outcome should be about both you and your networking partners gaining value. Also, ask questions to keep both you and those with whom you are networking participating in a healthy exchange of ideas, information, and, opportunities.

- **Track what your networking partners are saying.** Focus on listening deeply to gain an understanding of what matters most to your networking partners.

- **Put the desires and any requests of those with whom you network into your mental filing cabinet.** When you take the time to take note of what matters to your networking partners and then look out for connections and opportunities for them, you set into play a significant *spirit of reciprocity* to receive the same as you give.

- **Look for connection points.** For example, if you were both from Texas, you can build on this connection. Try this even with people you already know. You will be surprised that you will very likely discover things you didn't realize you had in common. For example, Melissa was recently with a colleague she had known for years and they both just discovered they were originally from Cleveland.

- **Get to the point where you ask, "How can I helpful?"** Be prepared to take some time with this step. It requires patience, as many people are not used to being asked this question. I usually have a sense of how I can help someone before I ask, but I ask anyway. Never assume.

- **Agree on your respective next steps.** Don't leave without these. Set a follow-up date for when you will reconnect and make a list of things you each will do to help one another. I leave with "Let's say connected on this!"

Achieving a quality network

As we strategically implement the science of networking, we should always keep in mind the art. This is where the human, intuitive side of things comes into play. Here are some thoughts to help you do just that:

- **Become an active listener.** Listen for understanding instead of for information. Your attention to your networking partner's needs and interests will help you create opportunities that can lead to even more and better networking exchanges.

- **Stay open to new ideas.** Appreciate the new information or different way of looking at things your network partners offer. Even if you don't agree with them, respect their opinions. Successful networking comes from being open to the different viewpoints and ideas others share.

- **Stay genuine.** Be authentic - people can feel that! Being prepared is great, but without sincerity and transparency, you have nothing. When you're genuine and sincere, you'll attract people to you who naturally want to help you. Become interested in others. Then find out what matters most to them and center your conversations around their priorities. In turn, share your priorities. Network with those who care what matters to you as much as they care about what matters to them. Again, we are recognizing the focus on the few, not the many. As Melissa points out consistently, "You are only as strong as your weakest link. Therefore, weed out those weak links in your network." Also add the sentence, By weak links we mean people who are takers who don't have the capacity or interest to give back. A vibrant network starts and sustains itself with people who care about connecting and then help others connect through thoughtful introductions.

Quantity vs. quality

You very well may start networking with a large number of people first, before you start trimming and/or weeding your network to pull out those few, quality connections. But focus on developing quality networks as soon as possible for optimum networking results. Here's a little quiz that will help you compare measures of your quantity *and* quality.

QUANTITY

Rate your current **quantity** of networking on a scale of 1 to 5 (1 being lowest, 5 being highest).

	Attending organization meetings to locate new referral sources
	Involving yourself in outside activities with others (e.g., sports, hobbies, meet-ups, professional organizations, religious activities)
	Making calls to new contacts to create referral source relationships
	Reading articles to identify influencers and potential connections
	Asking current contacts to create referral source relationships
	Spending time planning the development of your referral base

QUALITY

Rate your current networking **quality** on a scale from 1 to 5 (1 being lowest, 5 being highest).

	Attending organization meetings to locate new referral sources
	Involving yourself in outside activities with others (e.g., sports, hobbies, meet-ups, professional organizations, religious activities)
	Making calls to new contacts to create referral source relationships
	Reading articles to identify influencers and potential connections
	Asking current contacts to create referral source relationships
	Spending time planning the development of your referral base

Did you notice that the questions were the same for both quantity and quality? That's on purpose, so you can think about your network in terms of all its component parts. If your *quality* score was lower than your *quantity* score, you need to change your focus. A feeling of dissatisfaction can actually be a starting point toward building better networking skills. If you take action to improve your current status, it leads to change.

Your focus should be on building smaller, high-quality relationships, first. From there you can actually more quickly build significant numbers of relationships overtime. Why? It's because the more your network is made up of quality networkers who practice moving up the five levels of networking we pointed out earlier, you will have people who work better with you and as advocates for you and vice versa. It's always easier when everyone is conscious, thoughtful and deliberate around building quality relationships. So, the message here is to start small to grow big.

In the next chapter we'll explore what networks can look like to help you find the place where *preparation* meets *opportunity*.

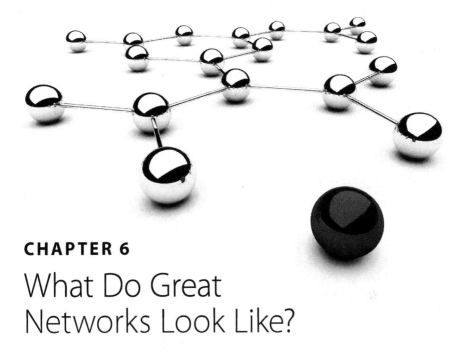

CHAPTER 6

What Do Great Networks Look Like?

No matter what industry you're in, membership in an organization is a good place to start to create a great network. These can revolve around your profession, but can also be social in nature, focused on sports, theatre, a gym, a cigar club—whatever is popular with men and women in or outside of your age group. Whether you're in your twenties or thirties, transitioning in your career, or getting ready to retire, find something you love to do and either join or create a network around it.

The power of creating your own network

Through the years we have both discovered that some of the best networks you can be part of are the ones you create yourself. For example, I'm passionate about golf. I moved from the middle of the city to the suburbs so I could live close to a golf course. It's something that I intentionally built into my lifestyle. I now belong to a golf club at which there are organized golf events, and I pay dues each year to be able to participate. But many of my friends are not members of golf clubs. I want to be able to play with my friends who are outside of the club on a regular basis. Because I'm a member, I'm able to bring them to my club to play.

What I've found is that most are not members of a golf club. They may play at various golf courses around Chicago, but they haven't committed to becoming a member of a club. I could play with random guys at my golf club, but I prefer to play with friends who are in different golf circles. I'm fortunate enough to have friends from all over the city of Chicago and beyond. Many of us enjoy golf, but it can be difficult to play regularly with one another when we don't live nearby, or if we already belong to country clubs in our respective neighborhoods. So I decided to create my own circle—the golfers from my network. I named it "Circle of Friends."

My friends and I came together for competitive golf but, through the years, the network has also found unique causes to support while still having fun and building friendships. Golf was the activity that connected us, and at the core it was men connecting around a passion for competition. The relationships grown in this network created new opportunities for all of us. Most of us have ended up doing business with one another but we also socialized beyond golf, attending each other's weddings, traveling together and getting to know each other's families.

The Circle of Friends has been in existence for fifteen years now. Of the seventy men from around the country in our club today, forty-five of them were not connected before I introduced them to this group. We hold six golf events a year. I initially funded the circle, creating my own golf network, but now the circle funds itself.

You can do the same thing to grow your own network, if not with golf, then with a group in your own profession or by starting a social circle focused on things like fantasy football, attending sports events, physical fitness pursuits such as running or scuba diving, or playing poker or—whatever you're into. It doesn't have to cost a lot. Work with what you have. If all you have is a backyard with a fire pit, then start there. Focus on putting people together to share, connect, and engage.

Taking your network to the next level through unique connections

Now, consider the individual networks of business owners and entrepreneurs who have created wealth for their families and communities. They can span twenty-five to fifty years. Here are attributes of some of the great networks we've seen over the years:

- They are intentional and deliberate.
- They have set goals.
- They know the imperative of practice and preparation.
- They work hard at what they do.
- They are determined, focused, and disciplined.
- They recognize their strengths.

- They embrace teamwork.
- They have overcome obstacles.
- They are competitive and know how to win.
- They are considered experts within their industry.
- They know how to be strategic and develop relationships.
- They invite those with whom they have commonalities and similar risks

Adapting to change

Although faced with a shorter career span than most occupations, NFL players have a unique skill set they've worked years to develop, just like entrepreneurs and the executives. But their challenge is to figure out how to translate their sports skills beyond the football field. For them to be great networkers they have to learn to use their current platform as football players to develop network-building skills and leverage their platform while they still have it.

There are some players who are good at developing their networks after football, whether in the broadcast booth, joining a company, coaching, owning a business, or becoming an investor. But the majority of players find they are not prepared for life after football. If you're thinking football is nothing like your situation, think again. Journalists, singers, celebrities, CEOs, and anyone in a position of influence or power who loses or leaves their position or company may lose their platform, making life more difficult.

For example, if you're a Chicago Bear, you can secure a meeting with just about anyone in the city of Chicago because you have positional power and influence. But this level of influence drops away when you're no longer a Chicago Bear. Now, you're *a retired* Chicago Bear. You've lost your positional influence of being a football player and therefore it becomes much harder to get people to listen to you.

But there are those players and others who took their future into their own hands, effectively reinventing themselves. Bo Jackson is a good example of someone who took such an opportunity to reinvent himself. When his football career ended after a hip injury in 1991, he didn't give up. He turned to baseball and to other ventures. He's been an entrepreneur, a banker, an actor, a TV spokesperson, and a sports pitchman, a philanthropist in the Chicago area. He's expanded his network and has been successful because he realized that he wouldn't always be a professional athlete.

So whether you are in sports or any other field, always be prepared to transition. To this end utilize all of your skills while you're in a place of influence and then translate your positional power into becoming a business executive or entrepreneur or other options, before retiring from football. This means making time for networking now and on a regular basis.

Creating connection hubs

I have kids, and a full-time job that requires travel. I sit on six nonprofit boards. I'm also a member of seven national organizations, and an active alumnus of two universities. I have five club memberships, and I currently mentor two young adults. So naturally, people constantly ask me how I am able to make time for building my networks.

Here's my process: I connect with individuals and organizations I am interested in and passionate about. Then I combined my interests and my daily work in search. Over time, I was able to create what we referred to earlier as connection hubs. These hubs have allowed me to leverage my networks so that those involved, including myself, benefit. By being efficient and deliberately attentive to your networking strategy of creating your connection hubs, you too can increase the return on investment of your time.

Build the right networks on the front end and then create your own connection hubs as mentioned earlier. Currently these are my hubs:

- LINK Unlimited
- Goodman Theatre
- Metropolitan Club
- Executive Leadership Council
- Circle of Friends
- Biggs Mansion

Connection hubs are those networks that you turn into wells of ongoing connections. Why? They have structure and are part of a group initiative where they benefit not just one person, but many, because they offer ongoing opportunities to all involved. These are limited only by your imagination or the imaginations of those with whom you currently network.

What are your connection hubs? If you haven't created any yet, it's time to start. The following are steps you can take:

- Identify existing organizations where you might be able to create a connection hub. Whether you start a committee as I have done, or a meetup group, an internal network in your organization, or even a social group, you are creating a place and an environment for ongoing networking. This is a much smarter move than what we term "ad-hoc networking" where it happens often as a last-minute decision to go to a networking after-work event.

- Build structure into your connection hub. You will hear more about my connection hubs in this book, but note that even my social hubs have structure. Structure gives the members of the group the continuity they seek to build trust in the hub and use it consistently, growing their relationship with the network. The more trust that is built in the hub, the better the outcome of networking inside it.

- Celebrate successes. It might sound trite, but the adage that success breeds success has been found to be true, according to a recent study conducted by Stony Brook University. In other words, if you celebrate your collective successes with those in your connection hubs, you create a footprint of success that has a strong possibility of creating more success.

To share an example of this last point, I go back twenty-five years to when I began a tradition that has continued to this day—and it all started as a celebration. I moved to Chicago in June 1990, and by New Year's Eve of that year, I had two dozen friends and acquaintances. My girlfriend at the time lived in Atlanta, and I was excited for her to visit Chicago so I could show her the city and introduce her to my new friends. Since I wasn't sure where to go for New Year's Eve, I decided to throw a party for my small network of people, none of whom knew each other.

Back in my early Chicago days, the thing everyone had in common was that they didn't know what to do with themselves on New Year's Eve. (Sometimes the common interests are a little more precise than that, I promise you.) So I threw a party and invited all my friends to my two-bedroom apartment. My Atlanta girlfriend was the opposite of me—more of an introvert. She worked for the Hyatt in management and was staying in one of their hotels downtown. She couldn't believe I was throwing this big party because all she wanted to do was spend time with me and had no interest in meeting new people, so she decided not to come.

Despite having told everyone about her for months and being somewhat embarrassed when she didn't show—everyone at the party had a great time. The next day, I dragged my friend, Thomas Harvey, to a New Year's Day party that he didn't want to go to. Fortunately, he went because I overheard a woman at the party talking about him as we walked by. I nudged him over and said, "You see that woman over there? She was telling her girlfriends that you have a nice butt." That was enough to empower him to go over and talk with her. As a result, they've now been married for twenty years. After that party, Thomas and I decided that we'd had such an amazing experience that we were going to spend New Year's Eve together every year. To date, we've only missed one New Year's in twenty-five years.

Through the years we have celebrated in Chicago, Phoenix, Washington and Dallas. Each time we meet, we invite new friends to our parties to network. Who would have known at the time we made our first strong connection (the fact that we had both just moved to Chicago and didn't know but a handful of people), that Thomas would meet his wife and that we would stay great friends, traveling the world, sharing many wonderful experiences.

CHAPTER 7
Building Your Brand and Your Brand Story

You have a brand story as an individual, apart from the one you have with your company. Your brand story is more expansive. It's actually more about *why* you have become who you are more than anything else. This question of why you are doing what you are doing now, stems strongly from the people you have met and built relationships with over the years.

Because of these relationships, opportunities emerged: you took job A or opportunity Z. You found yourself traveling the world, or living someplace you never thought you would live. Your unique connections created the story you now share with others when they ask, "How did you get to where you are today?" And, for better or worse, you have a story that has emerged from your connections. This is your *brand story*.

Melissa and I have been building our networks and our brands and our brand stories over the past three decades. Here is an overview of my network path, encompassing ten positions in the following organizations:

- Central Michigan University
- Michigan State University
- United Airlines
- Motorola
- Deloitte
- Monster Worldwide
- Hudson Highland Group: Hudson Inclusion Solutions
- Viacom/MTV Networks
- Heidrick and Struggles

With each step in my journey, I've benefited from my network, and each person within my network has, more often than not, also benefited. As managing partner in charge of the diversity advisory practice at Heidrick, I share my brand story daily. It's now a seamless part of my life now and it all starts with *how* I network.

Remember I shared at the beginning of this book how my mom sat my brother and me down when I was only thirteen, and told us that we would be on our own when we reached eighteen? I took her very seriously and started thinking about my future and what was possible for me as I approached the end of my senior year in high school.

Based on who was in my network then, my career possibilities came down to three options:

- Get a job in Detroit (rather than a career), like my other family members.
- Consider joining the armed services. A number of people I knew had served nobly, and that was a respectable option.
- Further my education by attending college. It was the least probable of the three options because at that time I didn't know anyone who had attended college.

My preferred plan was to attend college and find a career. It became my Plan A, but I always had a Plan B in mind—to go into the armed services. I had gone so far as to visit my local Army recruiting office where I was given an overview of the enlistment process. When the presentation was over, the officer in charge told me to come back and officially enlist when I was ready.

I never told anyone about Plan A. In my youthful exuberance, even though I had limited knowledge of what a college career would entail, I was fairly confident my top option would work. I held this stable optimism that college was possible for me. Not knowing anyone who had gone to college and graduated, I had no reference as to what to expect, or how to apply. I wasn't even sure I was college material. In retrospect, this was a blessing because I didn't know anything different. I just thought, *"Why can't I go? Why not me?"*

My strategy was to apply to college and make something happen. I didn't tell anyone because if it didn't work out, no one would know that I failed to get in. This was the first time I tried a strategy for my career. I knew you had to submit an application that included a $30 processing fee. I ended up applying to sixteen colleges. I had a part-time job bussing tables and washing dishes at a restaurant that paid me $65 a week. I ended up using half my weekly paycheck for money orders to send in with my college applications.

Before I knew it, I had applied to sixteen different colleges and had received rejection letters from every one of them. (By the way, I still have all 15 letters.) Despite this setback, I wasn't completely discouraged, because one of the letters ended with, "If you would like to discuss this decision, please call us for an appointment." Strangely, I immediately felt this was a little crack in the door for me, offering an opportunity I was ready to seize.

Right away, I called the university to set up an appointment. My family didn't have a car, so I asked a close friend, Rick, if he would drive me to Saginaw Valley, two hours away. He replied right away, "You're my guy. Let's do it!"

It was a bright spring morning that the two of us skipped school without telling our parents and set off on our journey. I distinctly remember stopping at a gas station, and after giving Rick $25 for gas, I had enough left over to buy a map that we unfolded and carefully spread out on the hood of Rick's car. We carefully planned our road trip.

We arrived at the parking lot of the school, where I quickly changed into my only suit. It was made of black wool, not quite right for this exceptionally warm spring day. Rick said a prayer for me, and then I headed into the admissions office. I met with the associate director of admissions and her first question to me was, "Where are your parents?" I told her they were at work (which wasn't true). My mother didn't have a job at the time and my father wasn't even active in my life.

Then she asked, "How did you get here?" I replied, "My buddy drove me." She smiled warmly and ushered me into an adjacent room. But then it came time for me to show her my transcripts that showed all Cs—only a 2.5 GPA. My philosophy in high school had been to *just do enough to get by*. I thought as long as you had passing grades, you could get into college.

After a few minutes the director said, "Mr. Dexter, there's nothing I see that would give me any indication that you would be successful here."

But I didn't want to give up. I told her, "I don't think these transcripts tell my story accurately. I know if you give me a chance, I could be successful. I would like the chance to show you."

She responded, "I'm sorry. I can't help you."

Feeling defeated—remember I had been already turned down by fifteen other schools—I got up and started to leave. Suddenly she said, "Wait a minute. You made the effort to be here. I owe it to you to see if the admissions people might reconsider and we need to exhaust all options."

I was over-the-top excited, but she then she added, "Mr. Dexter, please listen. This does not look good, but I will see what we can do. You'll see a response in the form of a letter in two to three weeks." (There was no e-mail back then).

When I got back in the car, my buddy asked, "How did it go?" For some reason, I was optimistic. We drove home. No one had even realized we'd been gone, and we kept the secret to ourselves. Every day, I would wait anxiously for the mail. I still had Plan B, so if this didn't work out, no one but Rick would ever know. I asked mom every day whether she had gotten the mail. She kept asking why. I ended up telling her I was waiting on a decision from a college, but she didn't really understand what that meant.

The following week I was still hopeful and then, one day, there it was a letter from the school. I could tell it was a slim letter. I'd already seen fifteen of those that had turned out to be rejection letters. Yet, I still eagerly opened the letter in our basement where no one would see me, wanting privacy in case it was bad news. After tearing open the envelope, the first thing my eyes settled on was the line:

"Congratulations, you have been accepted to Saginaw Valley State University on a probationary status. You are allowed to take 12 credits and if you get a C average we will then consider you for full admission." It was a day I have never forgotten.

By year-end, I had become good friends with my seven white roommates. I also got involved with student government, the Fellowship of Christian Athletes, and made the track team.

Reflections and pointers

I had no idea a single decision to call the university, skip school and drive up to Saginaw would change the trajectory of my life, my family's life, and the networks I would be involved with the rest of my life. This was the first time I had really challenged myself and taken a risk. This pivotal event became the foundation of my whole career. But I didn't realize the ripple effect until many years later.

Now I see the results of my actions and how a single act and the connections I made as a result could make all the difference in my future and how my actions help to build my brand story.

Tips

- Here is an insight from my good friend, Kevin Newell. When Kevin was Chief Brand Officer for McDonald's he reminded his franchisees and staff often that your brand is what your customers say it is not what you say. So in order for customers, in this case people within the network, to articulate your brand in the manner you desire there are very specific behaviors you must project. You first have to determine what you want your brand to be known for and this has to be very intentional. Everything you do should feed and nurture that brand perception. For young professionals, especially, it's very important that they establish a credible reputation as they start to build their networks.

- Really understand that the right connections make the difference. Find even one *right* connection for your network as soon as possible.
- Don't wait for someone else to make connections for you. Take charge.
- Don't stop until you get to the "yes." I had sixteen nos before I got a yes. Persevere.
- Stay optimistic. If you're not optimistic about your career, who will be?
- Start your plan early. Be deliberate and intentional.
- You can always change course, but you need to have a plan.

Building my brand story

Along with all of these new experiences, I was developing new connections, new friends, and meeting different types of people. I loved every minute of it. And, just as my story of my challenges getting into college became an integral part of my brand story, so did my first summer job following that pivotal growth year.

It happened right at the end of my first school year. A recruiter from Cedar Point Amusement Park was visiting our campus to discuss summer jobs for students. After hearing that I would be able to get room and board and a summer of meeting all kinds of new people from all over the Midwest and living in Sandusky, Ohio, I wholeheartedly decided to sign up.

I had no idea that this decision would help me lay the foundation for my networking success. The experience helped me get more comfortable with taking risks and meeting new people. After having made it through my first year with over 4,000 college students, I was now in a group of twenty somethings from all over the Midwest that summer of 1980. I was assigned to work in Ride Operations, where I was trained to be an operator on The Sky Ride, the monorail that moved throughout the park. I lived in the dorms on the property in Sandusky, Ohio.

I didn't know one person there, but I was excited about the adventure. I was twenty years old and assigned to a dorm room with seven other roommates—four bedrooms with two guys in each room. We also shared a kitchen and bathroom. But we had to figure out how to get along. In most cases I was the only African American. So I had no choice but to find ways to connect. Early on this experience allowed me to practice networking and building my connection skills.

We had to figure out among us how to buy groceries, make meals, and live together. I didn't drink and all my roommates loved to drink and smoke. But that was OK. We were all committed to doing our jobs at the park and then hanging out together at night. I remember when we would return to our dorm room after a long day's work. I would look at us, all in different-colored uniforms, as we worked in various sections of Cedar Point, but see how we all connected around our workdays we bonded.

So I took the skills I learned during that summer back to Saginaw Valley in my second year. They helped me greatly. I was now, more than ever, at ease developing friendships. I went on to work at Cedar Point for the next two summers, and I still have friends from that time. I have gone to weddings of people I worked and roomed with and to this day, I look back on those skills that I developed and appreciate that experience. Serendipitously, Melissa also worked at Cedar Point we later discovered as we shared the stories of our career development and early years.

Right before I went back to school, I returned to Detroit. All I heard that week was, "Who the hell *are* you? You're not the person we knew!" I'd left as a 17-year old street kid from Detroit. A year later I returned as "Mr. Preppy" with a pink shirt, a V-neck sweater, and brown penny loafers. My friends and family members tried to conduct an intervention on me because they felt I was too comfortable now in the so-called "white world." We laughed about it, but they thought they had lost me. I had become open to new experiences that gave me options, and I had begun to think in a different way and to make different choices. I had also developed a confidence in myself in meeting new people and embracing new experiences.

Because of my efforts at school and those summers spent at Cedar Point, today you can put me in the whitest of white environments, and I'll quickly figure it out and find my way. Incidentally, that's probably the number one struggle for African American corporate executives—the navigation in a mostly, or all-white environment.

If you look at my track record within every organization I've been a part of, most people would say, "Man, how did you manage to get to do all of that, knowing that you're one of only a handful of blacks?"

But I think it was because of my experience—something I've become really good at—downplaying who I was at work, and up-playing the guy who fits in and who can navigate different cultural waters.

Something I learned early on from Cedar Point as that as much my white roommates had our differences, there were always things we had in common. At Cedar Point we all had a common, positive work ethic. Looking back thirty years, I can see I didn't recognize the science behind this, but I intuitively grasped the same concepts Melissa has seen in action during her years working with various companies. I was just trying to figure out how to survive there. It was in survival mode that I began to develop my own process of connecting. I had no idea I would continue to develop my process throughout the next twenty-plus years.

I also learned how to creatively connect with thousands of new people, daily, at Cedar Point. There, I had to be "on" constantly, helping them as much as possible. The combination of science and art came together to form my brand, my story, and my process of networking.

A turn of events

When I returned to college the next fall, I was thirty-eighth in line for a dorm room. In other words, I had no place to live. On top of that, my financial aid didn't come through because of a technicality: I hadn't filled out the forms completely. There were only two days before the semester was to start! This led to another fateful meeting with the head of financial aid, Paul Gill. After I explained my situation, Paul suggested I go back to Detroit to get myself together and return the next year.

I retorted, "That's not an option." I had saved $1,200 from my summer working at Cedar Point. And though I had $800 to make the first payment for classes, I still didn't have a place to stay. Luckily I found that a local community college, Delta College, had a dorm room open, which I was able to make a deposit using the rest of my savings. Delta was nearly six miles from Saginaw Valley and back then there was no transportation between the two campuses. So every morning I ran the distance down a two-lane, dusty country road to campus.

When I got there, I would shower and change into the school clothes I had stashed in my buddy's dorm room. At the end of the day, I would change back and run home at dusk or later in the dark. I ran with a stick just in case I happened on a stray dog or coyote. I remember that semester in my life like it happened yesterday. It keeps me grounded in my life as I always remember that at any time things can get rough, but it's your commitment to staying with what you started and working through the challenges that builds character and discipline. That time in college represents the cornerstone of my networking discipline. Just as I didn't give up when the going got tough, I don't give up on my commitment to value relationships and connections.

Creating one of my first networks that built my brand

Another way I started networking in college was by joining the track team, which was made up of primarily guys from northern Michigan, a part of the state I knew nothing about. I joined and became an integral part of a team of sixty men. In my sophomore and junior years, Saginaw Valley was the National Association of Intercollegiate Athletics (NAIA) National Champion. The most interesting part of those championships was that we won it without having an indoor track. Becoming a member of this team helped me find a wonderful sense of belonging. I came from an all-black neighborhood, and now, here I was with a team that was 98 percent white. We couldn't have been more different as our backgrounds and experiences were on opposite ends of a spectrum. As with my undergraduate roommates, and my Cedar Point roommates, I had to navigate this network *culturally*. We had some amazing experiences and built life-long friendships. And surprisingly, we were all recently inducted into the Cedar Point Hall of Fame.

My roommates listened to AC/DC and drank from beer kegs. This is where I learned that all white guys aren't the same. Just as there are many subcultures within cultures in the black community, there are subcultures within cultures in the white community. This revelation was new to me. There I was, again thrust into an entirely new environment where I had to quickly learn how to survive.

I had to figure out this new environment, try to make friends with my new roommates, find connecting points, and be open to having new experiences. The first thing I did was make sure my roommates were comfortable with *me*. Most of them had never roomed with a black guy before. It was an eye-opener for them too. There were more of them than of me, so early on, it was one-sided. I hung out with the guys, listened to their music, and tried to understand what was important to them. I didn't drink or smoke, and they thought that was very weird, but because they were comfortable with me they accepted me anyway. Once again, some of my friends back in Detroit started to question my loyalties and were surprised at how comfortable I had become in this strange environment.

It was fun but it was also a tough time because I was trying to work both sides of the fence. Some of the black women quickly crossed me off their dating lists because I was spending so much time with white people. Early on, it was about survival. After I got through that first year, I thought, "You know what? This is not bad. I can hang. I can be in different cultures." I made a strategic decision that I've always known was pivotal—that I could still be who I am as a person. I could be comfortable in different cultures. In fact, it became the foundation of my career.

If you currently have a similar challenge as I did and Melissa has, think about ways you can connect, not because you have to but because you can. And if you do connect, we believe you will leverage your career and/or new business opportunities in ways that will surprise you. It's not easy but it could be very worthwhile.

Show how your networking brand will help others

Another step in building out your brand story is showing how your brand will help others build their own networks. I do this by consciously holding networking meetings regularly. To this end, I usually meet with five to ten people weekly, and spend thirty minutes at the front end of each one. I let those in my network know that I'm open to having conversations with just about anyone they refer to me for thirty minutes. My goal is to give these referrals enough of my time to hear what they're seeking to achieve in their lives, again, as I've said before, to discover a top priority for their work or professional lives they currently hold.

If a connection is made, and I know that I can be helpful, then I want to sustain that connection. It's just part of who I am and how I operate. I can always make time for a short phone call or a cup of coffee, especially if I know that the other person is looking forward to it. Even if I have no idea where this will lead or what the topic is, I know that during that thirty-minute conversation, I'll ask, "So how can I be helpful?" And if I can be helpful and the connection is made, I'll be there. If I can't be helpful, I will let them know and try to connect them with someone else to whom I think can be helpful.

Kim is a member of another one of my networks, the Executive Leadership Council (ELC). She recently retired as the comptroller from a Fortune 500 company. In her well-planned retirement, she wanted to get on a board. I told her that I would make some connections for her. I mentioned that I am the co-chair of the corporate board initiative for ELC, and knew of some things she could plug into. She was vacation bound and I said, "Once you get back from Hawaii, do you want to have a cup of coffee sometime to talk about your strategy?"

She agreed that we would stay in touch. I would find thirty minutes to meet her for coffee and see how I could be helpful to her thinking through what's next. When we met, I shared the example of John Deere's two new board members. And I said, "You know the only reason I bring this up is because Demetri and I started this conversation the same way three years ago. We met at an ELC event, just like you and I did, and look where we are now." She beamed and said, "I knew I got the right guy for this."

How to develop your networking brand

If I were to pinpoint when I started developing my networking brand it would be when I arrived in Chicago in 1990. I didn't know anyone here and I was blown away by the metropolis. I felt like a kid in a candy store—so many people to meet, things to experience, and explore. I was excited to learn more, always open, and wanted to share my new experiences. I think that's attractive to people.

How are you introduced?

A person with a strong networking brand would:

- Be receptive.
- Know how to leverage the connection to make it mutually beneficial.
- Know to lead with helping the person who was introduced.

One Saturday night after a Make-a-Wish Foundation formal dinner, a band was performing. I happened to be walking around the room during one of the songs and ran into an old friend who introduced me to a woman named Maria Castro, an executive at Comcast, whom Melissa had actually introduced me, by phone, earlier in the year. As a result of meeting Maria in person, I ended up connecting the executive directors of both Link Unlimited and the Goodman Theatre to be showcased on Comcast's TV show, *History Makers*. This was wonderful exposure for both organizations that make a big difference in Chicago and its surrounding communities. We call this a *win-win-win networking experience.*

My professional brand is different from my personal brand, but they're connected. I see combining them as a powerful networking tool. If I end my employment tomorrow, I won't have to restart my network. I've created networks around the things I'm most passionate about, not just my job or my industry. I don't have a start time or a stop time when it comes to networking. The power of my networks is that they're about helping people, not just leveraging my position or employment or title. I'm deliberate and strategic with:

- Making time for others.
- Leading with the question, "How can I help you?"
- Having both a short- and long-term payoff mentality.
- Incorporating networking into my everyday lifestyle.
- Developing actionable next steps.
- Spending time with people that are positive and add value to my network.

One of the most important things you must do to network effectively is to stay open to making connections. This is the foundation for success. It goes back to having a philosophy around networking with a focus on giving first.

In fact, money is only a by-product of your giving. If you lead with a focus on making money, you are transactional. If you give too much, you can go broke. In other words, giving requires discernment. I came to this concept more organically when I moved to Chicago. Specifically, I lived in a suburb of Chicago called Schaumburg, back then when there was little or no diversity in the suburbs. As one of the leaders of the Black Professional Network at United Airlines, my fellow colleagues and I started a monthly networking event at a place owned by the late Walter Payton called Club 34.

The event we coordinated once a month grew to include black professionals from other companies, growing to almost four hundred people. We kept the events going for several years. Those events were instrumental in helping us form connections that have lasted more than twenty years!

Tips

- Practice sharing your networking brand story or the genesis of your story with your current networking partners.

- Ask your networking partners to share their networking brand stories. As you help them create their stories, you will get more insights as to how to develop your story.

- Look at LinkedIn profiles of people with the same background as yours to see how they present themselves. As LinkedIn becomes more social with an edge around the *art* side of networking, we've seen profiles that very effectively share impactful networking brand stories.

- Take a sheet of paper and write at the top of it, "Why?" This is where you can start writing your networking brand story. Why are you doing what you are currently doing in your professional life? What made you choose the path you are on? How, after others helped or blocked you path to success? What is your vision for success? How could your network support your vision turning into a reality? All of these questions and your responses will help you develop your story.

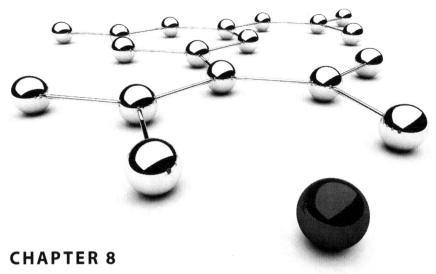

CHAPTER 8

Execute Your Best Play

Using the example of sports, let's say you're in a critical football game—a hard-fought game, something on the level of the Super Bowl. There are six seconds left on the clock. Someone calls a timeout. Everyone comes over to the huddle. There's time for just one more play. What happens?

In the background, each team assesses the situation. The opposing team has to play defense. The offensive team has a shot at scoring. They question whether they should do a pass or run the ball or kick for a field goal. Given the weather, what they've done in the past may or may not work. They take in all that information in two-minute timeouts and then they're left with one question—what's the best play?

So as I keep mentioning, my network is centered on helping people, and that often involves asking people to think about their best play.

For example, you've worked twenty years in your company doing marketing. That's the landscape. Now you want to go into technology. So we take in all the data. Then we can determine what your best play is currently. Based on what we see is that although you think technology is cool, you should stay in marketing for now. Get in there and make connections into technology. Could you go directly into technology? Sure. But that wouldn't be your best play. So, it's your turn. What's your best play? The philosophy is simple but it's really just taking in all the current data and determining your best play based on current situation and strongest probability to score.

Over the years I've had many people come back to me who remember our discussion around their *best play*. They say they have used it many times to coach others in the same way. In sitting and talking to senior executives at a crossroads in their careers, one of the things they say is, "Billy, I haven't been out there in awhile. I don't know how to get back in the game. I have not had to look for a job in twenty years."

I respond, "Not so fast. You've been a leader in your market segment. You've developed goals, milestones, and other metrics. You've managed dashboards that monitored performance. In fact, you've done that for billion-dollar organizations. You have a whole toolkit of talents. You just haven't used your set of tools to help you. So now it's time to figure out what's your business strategy. What's your goal? Focus your talents and experience now on you, not the company."

Then they get it. They need to do some research and ask, "How does my background and my *best play* prepare me for my *next* play?" Part of this includes asking, "Who are my connections—my relationships?"

Keep your focus on building a smaller quality base, first, to achieve sustainable success. Assess your networks to make sure your networking. Just like the seventy-five in my Circle of Friends golf group, there are about fifteen in my inner circle with five to ten in my core circle (or as Melissa calls it, your Power of Ten Circle). Check your networks to make sure they're vibrant. You've got to make contact with your connections regularly. It's about being empathetic to others.

Will's best play

My friend Will has a degree from Harvard. I met him over twenty years ago when he was a general manager at Baxter Healthcare. He was just starting his own business as an executive coach and we met to catch up. I suggested, "Why don't you add your coaching to the diversity practice I'm building? The coaches where I'm at are good, but wouldn't it be wonderful to have someone who has already taken the journey as an executive and has successfully managed to navigate the corporate journey? You've been where most people are trying to go. You've seen this journey through the lens of a diverse executive."

This step got Will his start in coaching. One of his clients is Orlando Ashford, the president of international cruise company, Holland America. Will has been working with Orlando for more than ten years. Ten referrals later, Orlando remains one of Will's great friends and has referred many others to him.

Orlando and I have been close friends for almost 20 years. Our stories, our networks and how we built our personal brands are among the strongest examples of "Making Your Net Work. There is no question, my relationship with Orlando is one of the most important relationships I have made and continue to nurture.

It all began when he was introduced to me by my wife, Gisel, who worked with Orlando at Motorola at the time. Gisel thought we should meet because she thought we had so much in common. Our initial meeting came as a result of being invited to a dinner party at Orlando's home. Being the networker that I am, I said, "Sure, I'm happy to go."

When we arrived at Orlando's house, he welcomed Gisel and she introduced me to Orlando. Then Orlando introduced his wife, Samantha, to Gisel and, what a surprise! Samantha and I quickly realized we knew already knew each other! We were immediately stopped on the porch and asked to explain how we knew each other before we were allowed to enter the party. After we all enjoyed a good laugh, I knew Orlando and I would become great friends.

Over the years we have developed many cross connections between friends, family, and coworkers. Orlando has not only been a friend, but a client, mentee, golfing partner, and neighbor. We have even traveled around the world for business and with our families. However, what I think we have the most in common is our commitment to valuing relationships and creating opportunities for others. We both have been very deliberate & intentional about developing our networks and by leading with helping others. As a result of us basically peer mentoring one another, we have created amazing opportunities for us as well as for many, many other people in our respective networks.

Manage how you show up: Dress for success

Connections and networking require a variety of skills. Believe it or not, taking care of your appearance can help you connect, or it can become a deterrent to great connections. I've always paid attention to my appearance. My dad was the sharpest dressed guy I ever met, and he told me a long time ago, "If you look good, you feel good." I believe there are certain things you can't control with regard to networking as to people's preconceived ideas about you, but there are many things you can control. Some of the important things you can control is your appearance. You can also control things like your eye contact (making sure to look people in their eyes but not stare), your handshake (using a firm, not weak or too strong grip), your stance (not shifting endlessly but confidently standing straight) and how you follow up with your network (reaching out regularly, not just when you need or want something).

There are certain things people think when they see an African American male or a blonde female, and not all of them are positive. We have a best-dressed contest in my Circle of Friends. Members of the group give away a beautiful trophy to the best-dressed person in the group each year. We want people to say, "These guys look good!" We actually give $5 citations to anyone in the group who shows up poorly dressed at any of our events. You don't want to be the guy who doesn't have it together! It's about how you show up personally and professionally.

When I'm with my buddies golfing, we're usually the only black guys on the golf course so we want to set a good example. It's the same when it comes to lifestyle. We want to build the element of care into our lifestyles.

> **Here are some wardrobe pointers to keep in mind:**
>
> - The first thing women notice about men is their shoes, so keep your shoes shined.
>
> - The first thing men notice about women is their nails, so keep your nails groomed and polished.

Much of my dressing success I owe to my tailor and friend, Haj. Not only is he my tailor, he's now also the tailor for many of my friends and colleagues because I introduced him through my network. Haj has been a great part of my network. Coming from austere beginnings in South Africa, he is now a very successful tailor who gives back to his community. He does this by taking the older suits of his clients, having them cleaned, and giving them to inner-city kids and young adults for their first job interviews. To this date, Haj has helped hundreds of young people get better starts in their careers.

Now it's important to know that I don't dress for anyone else. I dress well for me. Many people are conscious about their appearance. I believe it's incredibly important to career and business success You want your appearance to result in positive thoughts about you without you every saying a word. What you wear should always reflect a professional image and be appropriate for the occasion. Whether it is the fit, color or style of your clothing that stands out, remember that your appearance does indeed impact what people will think of you and how or even whether they will choose to network with you.

Finding your best play

So what will be your best play? Gather all of the best of your ideas, talents, and connections. Then turn them into a network of opportunity—your own connection hub, through purposeful, ongoing exchanges where you give and receive the best that you and your network have to offer. Don't worry if you're just starting with a small group of people because, remember, it's about the quality of your connections and then the focused time you take to learn to have vibrant, mutually beneficial exchanges. In other words, everyone's best plays benefits you and your best play benefits them.

Tips

- Make sure your appearance is appropriate for the occasion.
- Be mindful of the art, color and style of your outfit and whether it is appropriate for the culture.
- Plan out what you are going to wear and the impression you want to leave so you're not pulling together an outfit at the last minute.
- Make an investment in quality fabrics. Don't be afraid of building a custom wardrobe and/or asking for help from a stylist or tailor.
- Create a style or image and build your wardrobe around it. Whether it's wearing a red bow tie or a unique silk scarf to events, create a signature style that helps you stand out in a room.

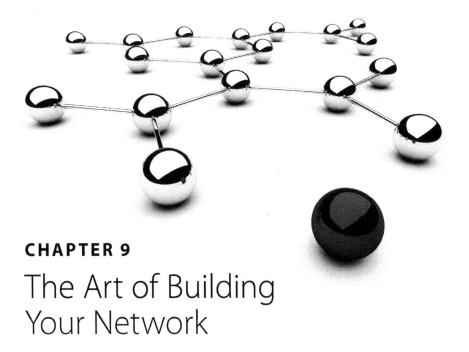

CHAPTER 9

The Art of Building Your Network

My good friend, Roger Crockett, is one of the best golfers I know. He is both methodical and technical. Those are great skills to have as a golfer, but at some point you have to *feel* the club and just put the club on the ball. Now I don't have the mechanics. I don't have the beautiful swing, but we can still compete with one another. I'm more about the *feel* of it. I say to myself, "Translate what you *feel* into that swing and trust it, Billy."

It was June a couple of years ago and Roger and I were out golfing. At this point we had probably played seven to ten times together that season. This time he was struggling—even with that beautiful swing. I thought to myself, "Great! I'm beating him." But after I beat him I saw he was still struggling. I couldn't take it anymore because he kept hitting crazy shots. This time he pulled it to the left. I retorted, "Roger, just *hit* the ball. You know how to play the game. Dude, you're thinking too much. Put the club on the ball. That's all you need to think about. Don't think about anything else. Just worry about taking that club you have and hit it on the center of the ball."

He proceeded and hit the ball *right down the middle*. Then he hit it *right down the middle* a second time. He kept doing this until the end of the round, and then did that game after game. A couple of weeks went by and we were once again playing and he said to me after, hitting the ball right down the middle once more, "Billy thanks so much for helping me just be in the here-and-now, and focus."

When it comes to golf, a golfer masters the fundamentals—the mechanical and technical—when they've got everything moving the right way. The intuitive golfer, who plays by *feel*, may be competitive. But in golf when it comes down to it, what prevails is the mechanics. It's the technical aspect of doing things the *right way* at the *right time*. I envy that mechanical and technical skill Roger has, but I also know I can break that complexity down into the simplest form—that is, putting the club on the ball.

Be here now

My top suggestion for "being here now" is particularly where you need to go when you're networking. It's about being an active listener, which is a key part of the *art* of networking. Nine times out of ten, networking comes down to deep listening.

When I connect the concept of being here now to networking, I *feel* my way through it. I don't necessarily have the science part of it down pat, but I've been learning through our sessions. I know my strength is that when I *feel* my way through things, it works for me. It may not be your style, but it's mine. Because it's me, and because it's authentic, people experience my networking as real and authentic. This helps me make deeper, more lasting connections.

I would argue that success in networking comes down to more of the art than science side. This is where it gets scary for some folks. This deepness, this "professional intimacy" as I call it, is almost spiritual, or at least reverential. The reverence is the feeling part. We've slowed down and listened to one another. We've been vulnerable and real. Some folks back off at this part of the process. For me, I don't compromise on the process. For example, last week at a networking event someone came up to Haj and said, "I've been trying to meet this guy, Billy Dexter."

Haj responded, "Billy Dexter? He's right over there. I'll introduce you."

So he introduced me. This guy just stood there while all these other people came up to talk with me. He just kept waiting patiently.

Finally, everyone else left. I was ready to turn and get a drink when Haj jumped back in and introduced me to this guy, who we'll call Jeff. I turned and gave Jeff my full attention. I said I would love to spend some time with him. I reached into my pocket and pulled out my card and gave it to him. I said, "Look, I'm really looking forward to connecting."

Fast forward a week or so. Jeff and I are sitting in Starbucks. I discovered that he was a graduate from Northwestern and had sent me his resume. He wanted to know whether he should get his MBA. He then jumped into sharing what he'd done with his career thus far. He wanted to focus on his situation. He wanted to network with me and see how I could help him. But first I needed to make a connection—the feeling side of networking—the art. I slowed him down. I asked, "So where are you from, Jeff?"

It was tough to connect with Jeff as he kept racing through his story, but I patiently kept slowing him down. I had reserved thirty minutes for our conversation as I normally do. However, I decided to take more time, an hour and fifteen minutes in this case because of the tug of war going on. However, finally he gave up. I listened to him and took some notes. I discovered where he came from and why he had pursued his career. Then, while going through my questions, I asked him, "Do you mind if I give you some feedback?" He nodded.

I said, "Jeff, all I've heard is what you want. But how do you give back? What's your networking philosophy? Who's in your network?"

He didn't have answers for my questions. He realized he needed to figure out *how* to develop a connection first. Then he realized that he needed to be helpful. He shared his thoughts out loud. Now we were getting somewhere. We had started an exchange going when he let go of *telling* me what he thought I wanted to hear and instead started exploring some connection points—those things we had in common. We had moved beyond the business-school approach to networking. I had given him time. I had doubled the time. I had spent forty-five minutes on developing the connection and then fifteen to twenty on the exchange as to how I can be helpful, where we went back and forth.

What was beautiful about that exchange was that before we walked away Jeff turned to me and asked, "Billy, before we leave here, how can I be helpful to you?" I smiled and replied, "Just asking that question is a great start. We'll wait and see. Now you're in my network. Count me as a fan. I'm going to be as helpful as I can."

By the time I got back to the office Jeff had sent me an email where he shared that he had gotten more from our session than he had in business school. I felt honored to get that feedback. I also thought it was time well spent. I was glad I gave him the opportunity to be part of my network because he was beginning to realize how to go through the process effectively. It was rewarding to me because I stayed committed to the process.

The art of possibility

There's definitely the *science* side of networking—from the process side. Our research shows that the number one belief among top-performing networkers is that anything is possible. After years spent observing their behavior, top networkers see possibility. In other words, they don't limit themselves, or limit what's possible. The art side of networking is all about being open to possibilities. There are people who have provided us with great insights into creativity and how we can all tap into our inner creative selves.

We seem to live in a more creative time. Among our favorite thought leaders are Seth Godin and Steven Pressfield, the author of *The War of Art*. There's also Elizabeth Gilbert, who recently came out with her book, *Big Magic*. Consider Daniel Pink's *A Whole New Mind*, where he shares that he believes the talent of the future will be people who are more right-brain dominant. For this reason, I believe the art of networking fits with people who are creative—people who see many different connections.

Keeping an optimistic outlook creates connection opportunities

I always set out with expectations that good things will happen. At my core, I'm an optimist. Doing the right thing by people always comes back as a blessing. I think you always have to see possibility! For example, once on a flight from Chicago descending into Raleigh-Durham, North Carolina, you could hear the wheels of the plane struggling to come down. People were audibly concerned. Then the captain announced, "Right now, the back wheels are not coming down, but we have about forty minutes of fuel, so we're going to keep circling until they come down. Don't panic, but we're going to rehearse the crash position."

As we're going through this ordeal, everyone is thinking, "Oh my god. We're going to crash." But I immediately played out the scenarios in my head and thought, "If we crash, there's usually four or five people who survive. I'm going to be one of them." I just knew it. So while we practiced the crash position, I thought, "What is my escape route?" I just knew I was going to survive. I have no idea where that certainty came from. But I had an innate belief that I was going to survive, and good things would happen to me, like surviving a plane crash.

Luckily, the plane did not crash. The gear came down with only five minutes of fuel left. I didn't have to find out if I would be one of the sole survivors or not. What mattered was the belief that I held in my heart. It's that belief of having some sort of a successful outcome that helps me move through challenges.

Where does that belief come from? If I could tie it back to anything, it might be a part of my favorite quote, which I have framed on a poster at home. "If it is meant to be, it is up to me." That goes to show how through my journey, with the exception of God's blessing and favor, I have felt that it's been up to me. My approach has been that I can't count on anyone else. In my early years I thought that counting on someone else was a weakness because others could let you down.

I have grown from that point of view. If what I want is going to happen, I've got to figure out how to do it myself. When faced with a challenge, I've got to figure it out. Is there an obstacle in my way? I have to own it. As far back as I can remember, I've had the view that good, bad, right or left, it's on me. I have since learned that by having the right people in your network, you can depend on them because you have made strong connecting points,

By taking ownership and having that expansive belief that anything is possible, you will realize the best possible opportunities. Take time to regularly envision all the opportunities that may come from your networks. Then like me, you will be prepared to leverage your opportunities into connection hubs, as I've done with organizations like the Executive Leadership Council, Chicago United, and the Goodman Theatre.

Be thoughtful and careful about the networks you build. Make every effort to create value for them and you will see strong returns on your investment of time.

Tips

- **Connect like-valued people and groups together.** This strategy is about you becoming the matchmaker. By being the connector you become that person everyone wants to know because you make things happen. You create opportunities because you brought the people together, so you stand out as someone others want to know. In turn, opportunities will come to you.

- **Be selective. Don't just throw two people or groups together.** Make sure there are leaders in each group who will work collaboratively for the good of both groups.

- **Test out your artful merging of networks with a small event.** Through the years both Melissa and I have created events that have brought us ongoing new business opportunities. But we also took our time building the initial events that were small, manageable, and filled with those from our networks who gave us feedback as to how to improve the next time. We kept improving our smaller events until the bugs were worked out and we could scale them.

- **Stay with your networked alliance of both groups to the point they're running smoothly.** In other words, be a good shepherd of each group.

- **Stay in touch as an advisor.** By staying connected with those whom you play the role of advisor (this would be the case with those you mentor), you have the opportunity to make an even greater impact on their lives.

- **Build your networks around your passions and interest.** When you are deliberate and intentional as you develop your networks and you build value-based relationships, you create a win-win for everyone.

- **Build personal, professional, social and community networks** that allow you to interact and develop connections that you would not normally connect with.

- **Work to establish strong connecting points with others as you network.** Keep returning to your commonalities as a good place to leverage and sustain your connections,.

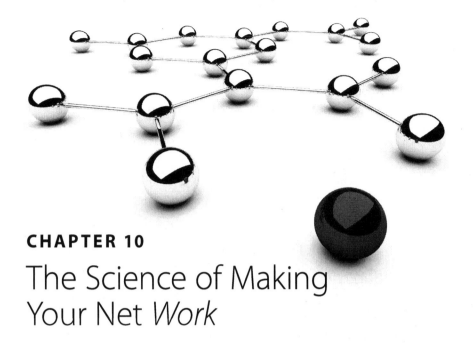

CHAPTER 10

The Science of Making Your Net *Work*

The best place to experience the science of making your net *work* is through what Melissa refers to as the Networlding Support Exchange (see below). It will help you get and sustain results for your networking partners and for you. Effective exchanges start with active listening. This can be done face-to-face or by phone. What matters is that you connect with your networking partners and discover things that matter to them.

Besides talking with your partners directly, you can see or hear what matters to them by reading and following what they discuss in social media, blogs, and/or in articles. By listening to people and not just waiting for a pause in the conversation where you can jump in with your own thoughts, you'll find out all kinds of ways to help others and, in turn, you'll create a spirit of reciprocity for them to do the same for you. Seek to find out what your partners find most exciting about their work and what they like to do in their spare time. What are their goals and dreams for the future? What are their current challenges?

Listening also involves creating a *balanced* networking exchange where you share what you need and your networking partner does the same. If both parties come together with this intention, they're more likely to create an ongoing exchange because both receive attention combined with support. This looks like asking how can we help one another rather than how can I help myself? We'll show you just how to master these exchanges later in this chapter.

Networlding Support Exchange

The following is an overview of the Networlding Support Exchange that Melissa has created and tested with more than ten thousand people, from professionals to entrepreneurs to students. This model is a hierarchy representing the various levels of support you can both request from and give to others when you network. However, we both suggest that you start by giving to your network.

Extensive studies on human networks show that you achieve better results when you have regular communication (called exchanges) with diverse people. The model below illustrates the hierarchy of the development of effective relationships.

Emotional support: Our feelings about others serve as the foundations for our relationships. The focus of exchanging emotional support with another is to create rapport, a relationship of mutual trust and affinity.

Information support: Information is a combination of messages. Once there's an initial rapport built, we then feel comfortable to share information of value. Information support helps you realize your goals.

Knowledge support: This level of support takes your networking to a new level as people combine the information that they acquire with their experiences. This support can provide you with both tacit knowledge (understood or implied without being stated) and explicit knowledge (suggested though not directly expressed).

Promotional support: As we continue to build rapport we naturally promote the attributes of our networking partners with others in our networks. This evolves into strong word-of-mouth marketing results.

Wisdom support: Wisdom support adds an element of selection and prioritization to the things we share with those in our network.

Transformational opportunities support: A natural result of moving up the ladder of support for our networking partners. With ongoing exchanges of support comes the evolution of opportunities that are much more robust than those that come from traditional networking.

Community support: As you and your networking partners realize transformational opportunities, it's now time to pay your blessings forward. Reach back to your networks and those communities you support or new communities you can now support.

Initiate a support exchange

Use the Support Exchange to start the process of building effective relationships through effective conversations. An effective conversation with someone you're just meeting starts with questions that speak to the interests and needs of that person. Throughout this book, the stories we share will relate to networking exchanges on various levels of this model.

Find out first what matters currently to those in your network and then direct your conversation with them around those things. This focus on your networking exchanges will help you grow a stronger, lasting foundation for ongoing networking opportunities. Finally, practice will make a big difference in building your skills and ease of this model.

The following are all the levels of the Support Exchange with each level providing questions you can ask to start vibrant conversations that lead to networking success:

Emotional support questions

- What brought you here today?
- What's going on in your professional life right now that really excites you?
- What one project are you working on that is most interesting?
- "What is it about this organization that you like most?"
- What other groups are you involved with that you really like?

For people out of work

- What type of job are you looking for that would be even better than the one you just left?
- What about your old job made you the happiest?
- What's the most emotionally satisfying project that you have worked on?

Informational support questions

- What's the last good business book you read?
- What types of organizations are you interested in getting involved with?
- What industries are you most interested in?
- What kind of information would you like on specific businesses?
- What is one of the best ideas you learned in business recently?
- What are a few of the best information resources you have found?

Knowledge support questions

- What three ways could my clients (or customers) benefit from your services?
- What area of expertise don't you have that you would like to get more experience in?
- What is one area of your career or business you would like to develop that you're not currently developing?

- What is most exciting about your experience in your area of expertise?
- What is new in your field that others might not know?

Promotional support questions

- What are your top three strengths that you would like others to know about?
- What would you like people to say about you?
- What have past clients or business partners said is unique about you?
- Which of your last, few, successful projects were the most exciting?
- Which two people would like to have known more about you?
- What three or four organizations would you like to know more about you and your work?

Wisdom support questions

- What's one of the most important things you have accomplished in your professional life so far?
- What is a top piece of wisdom you regularly impart to others?
- What's one of the wisest things you have heard someone else say? Who said it?
- Who is a wise person you admire a great deal in history or business? Why?

Transformational opportunities questions

- What is a pie-in-the sky wish for you? How might this become a reality?
- What transformational outcome did you take part in or lead?
- What transformational outcome did you not participate in, but wish you did? Why?
- What one thing haven't you done yet in your career that you wish you could do?
- If you were to have the most successful year you have ever had, what would have happened?
- What three people do you think are transformational leaders and why?
- What three people would you like to work with on a transformational opportunity and why?

Bonus questions

- Who is one of the influential people you've had some kind of relationship with?
- What is one of the best pieces of advice you have ever had? Who gave it to you?
- Who is one of the most fun professional executives you have ever worked with?
- Which of your co-workers have you most admired, and why?
- What project or initiative are you most excited about currently, and why?

- Who is the most empowering boss you have every worked with? What have they done or said to empower you?
- What is your proudest accomplishment on an accomplishment of a project you partnered on?

Those are a lot of questions to keep in mind, but the more you ask them, the more a part of you they become. The secret is to be genuinely curious. You'll be surprised at how much you learn listening.

Tips

- **Create a balanced networking exchange.** Life's lessons keep bringing us back to this truth. You don't benefit in the end when you take much more than you give. The same is also true when you give much more than you take.

- **Try asking your current networking partners the question, "How can I help you?"** By offering your insights, you might discover opportunities that you didn't realize were possible to use your expertise to help them and perhaps also help the companies they come from. Melissa had a number of participants, for example, in her networking workshops, who explored using this question with neighbors they had never before had networking conversations with and, upon this question, were very surprised to find unique opportunities for new work emerge.

- **Become a networlder.** A networlder, unlike a networker, has ten or fewer key people who become networking partners in what is termed in social science, a primary circle. These partners regularly exchange emotional support, information, knowledge, promotional support, as well as leads and referrals for new business or career opportunities. The focus of networlding is on building mutually beneficial exchanges with like-minded and like-valued people

- **Spend 80 percent of your relationship-building time with your primary circle.** Melissa calls this the Networlding Circle of Ten. Once you have found those ten or fewer great networking partners and start having regular exchanges, you will achieve better results than networking with others who are not ready, willing, or able to have these exchanges with you.

How Melissa built her network

Here, Melissa shares her story of how she strategically built her network:

> I remember my days in Schaumburg—another commonality Billy and I have in common. I was married with two young sons. My husband traveled regularly and so I had to hire babysitters to help me because when we moved to the Chicago area from Ohio, I had transferred law schools and still had two years to go.
>
> After I finished law school back in 1987, I spent about six months at a large Chicago law firm. Less than a year later I got the entrepreneurial bug (most likely the result of growing up

with our house attached to my dad's florist shop and years of working all major holidays and taking orders daily). I decided to start my own company, a referral service that was like an early "Angie's List." I built my business up to five employees and then realized it was too much for me to handle. I had a husband who, very sadly, started having nervous breakdowns. I found myself needing to be with our two younger sons more and more. Those were tough years, but my network made it easier. Because I had grown up in my entrepreneurial family where I went with my dad to Lion's Club and other community gatherings, I had been exposed to networking at an early age.

Back then only 17 percent of all women owned small businesses. Today that number is 50 percent or more. It was just the beginning of women starting and growing significant companies. Within three years of starting my business, I had begun teaching entrepreneurship for the State of Illinois. This got me thinking about writing books.

I had taken every writing class in undergraduate and graduate school, where I taught composition while getting my master's, and later on in law school. I remember being told by one teacher, "You're either going to write one book and be done or you'll write many." I liked the idea of writing many books. That's where I began.

My first book was a resource book for entrepreneurs. I specifically focused it on starting a business in Chicago. This book got a lot of attention, particularly with banks and accounting firms. I started getting calls by professionals at some of those firms wanting me to come and speak or consult with them. Within a year I was asked to take a part-time position at a top Chicago accounting firm that also owned a training company for other accountants around the country.

I started teaching accountants how to network, and over the next two years, I taught hundreds of them to do so more effectively. At the time, there were only about four experts in networking in the entire country. I had published my first book on entrepreneurship through Dearborn Publishing, which later became Kaplan Publishing. My editor kept asking me what I wanted to write next. Of course, the obvious answer was a book on networking. So my second book, *Make Your Connections Count,* was all about my experience and insights around networking. I had a wonderful group of professionals around me to test out theories I had about what worked or didn't work when it came to building one's network.

Once that book was published, I kept going, writing more books on building alliances and knowledge networks. The years passed by and I kept writing. It was after my sixth book that my editor at my current publisher, Jossey-Bass, asked me what I wanted to do for my *next book.* I asked him to give me some time to think about that.

At this time, I was divorced and now helping my two sons through college. I was struggling both emotionally and financially, but I needed to keep working to make sure my kids got good educations. My net was working for me, though. Through my network I was asked to sit on the women's business advisory board at the University of Chicago. I was honored to be asked to be on the board, and was even more honored when they kept me on the board for several years. They also regularly asked me to present on panels around networking. But the most life-changing moment of being on that board was meeting Jocelyn Carter Miller, the co-author of my seventh book.

Jocelyn, a graduate of the University of Chicago, had just opened up the Latin American market for Motorola. I was introduced to her and asked her, "What's one thing in your life you haven't done yet that you would like to do?" Jocelyn, a beautiful black woman who had an undergraduate degree in finance and an MBA in marketing from the University of Chicago, replied spontaneously, "I would like to write a book."

I had been introduced as an author, but I was still surprised. I didn't expect her to say anything close to that. But I took her reply seriously. I told her I would think about what she said and get back to her as I had an editor who was always looking for new authors with good book ideas. But what Jocelyn and I talked about that evening centered on her interest and the recognition of the importance of networking in the corporate world.

Up until that moment, all of my experiences had been in the entrepreneurial world. Yes, I had connections into banks and accounting firms and even law firms and government, but I did not have connections into corporations, especially companies the size of Motorola, which at that time had eighty thousand employees globally. But the more I thought about the opportunity that could come from Jocelyn sharing her insights around corporate networking and me sharing my insights from the world of the small to midsize business and the entrepreneurial world, the more I knew the collaboration would be good. It occurred to me that maybe this could take my business to a whole new level. Maybe this would be my path out of my financial struggle.

The next day I put in a call to my editor, Cedric Crocker, at Jossey-Bass. Cedric was going to be in town and said he would like to meet and talk further about the new book idea I had. I remember that day, sitting in a cozy Italian restaurant on Rush Street. I shared with Cedric, "I have an idea about a new networking book. It would blend my last seven years of knowledge coaching, training, and consulting on networking with accountants, bankers, and entrepreneurs with professionals in the corporate world. I was ecstatic when he responded, "That's a great idea. What would you title the book?" I had no clue, I told him, but I would get back to him as soon as possible to offer up my top suggestions.

Cedric agreed to publish the book without a proposal, something that made my job a lot easier. I also knew we would be getting an advance and that would be helpful given the fact that, now, as a single mom, life was getting steadily harder and harder to manage financially. With both of my sons in college I was continuously getting financial surprises. The idea of a new book coming out gave me some hope that I would be moving to a better financial state, at least within the next year.

Things started to improve as we began work on this new book. We came up with the name, *Networlding,* because we felt it gave the process of networking a more global focus. There were people teaching networking in other parts of the world, but as a world concept, networking was just getting started. This was before the advent of social media. LinkedIn didn't get its start until the fall of 2002, Facebook didn't start until early 2004, and Twitter launched even later, in July 2006. So, even though *Networlding* was leaning future-forward in 1999 with a launch date set for fall 2000, we went with it.

During the time we were busy writing the book, Jocelyn had the honor of becoming Motorola's first chief marketing officer. That career development for her was beneficial for the book because it started the process of waking up the corporate world to the benefits of networking. And I loved the folks at Motorola. Engineers mostly, those employees were by far the best people with whom I could possibly share the many years I had now under my belt teaching people how to network more effectively.

As top engineers, they were great listeners. So when I shared my seven step process to them they followed all the exercises diligently and with great appreciation. I remember one event I was asked to present at where I was able to work with 350 of their top employees, mainly people from their women's network, but the event was open to others in their Schaumburg corporate offices.

I came up with two exercises that got them all involved in learning the concept of six degrees of separation, mentioned near the beginning of this book, that we all are five or fewer connections through introductions away from any other person in the world. This concept was originally presented in a short story by a Hungarian writer named Frigyes Karinthy in 1929, and popularized in an eponymous 1990 play by the same name written by John Guare, an Irish-American playwright. It was Guare who cited Guglielmo Marconi, an Italian inventor and engineer who lived from 1874 to 1937 as the initial person who proposed this concept.

Then in the 1960s, Stanley Milgram, a Holocaust survivor and a professor of social psychology at Harvard and Yale, conducted research on the concept.[12] His so-called "small world experiment" validated the six degrees concept, which grew in popularity through the years, including such spin-offs as "six degrees of Kevin Bacon."

But what has happened since 2003? In February 2016, Facebook's data science team found that the average number of degrees of separation between users was 3.57. The lowest degree of separation averaged at 2.9 and the highest averaged at 4.2."[13]

---

12 Stanley Milgram, "The Small World Problem," *Psychology Today*, May 1967.
13 Alejandro Alba, "Facebook Celebrates 12th Birthday, Shatters 'Six Degrees of Separation' Theory," *New York Daily News*, February 4, 2016, http://www.nydailynews.com/news/national/facebook-

There's also an app you can use to determine your degrees of separation: https://www.facebook.com/DegreesApp/

So, back to the exercise. We focused on their choice of what we called "Six Degrees of Caroline Kennedy." Here, I asked the 350 attendees to gather into groups of ten. Then I instructed them to share whether they knew Caroline; if they did, how they knew her; or if someone they knew was connected to her, who that person was. I gave them fifteen minutes to discover their degrees of separation from Caroline and then return to their seats.

I then asked participants to come up to the microphones up front to share their stories. Lines formed quickly. The sharing started with the first person stating, "I have a cousin in ballet class with Caroline." Then another stated, "My aunt used to work with Caroline."

The stories kept coming and I had to move them along, so I said, "OK, there are definitely a number of you who are within six degrees of Caroline. How about if everyone just stands up if you're within six degrees from her? To my surprise (as they say, you can't make these things up), two-thirds of that room stood up. Then everyone started looking around the room realizing their discovery. Just like the experiment by Milgram, we were experiencing a small world.

---

shatters-degrees-separation-theory-article-1.2520335.

After this exercise I continued explaining my process and then ended my presentation with one more exercise. This time it was for the attendees to gather again in groups of ten. I asked them to gather with people they had not yet met. Because Motorola, as I said, had eighty thousand employees at that time, I could pretty much count on the reality that there were people they had yet to meet.

The team at Motorola who put together the event had handed out notecards to each person prior to my presentation. For this exercise I wanted each group of ten and then each person in each group to put down one person they wanted to meet *inside* Motorola, someone they knew about but had yet to be introduced to, and then, one person *outside* of the company they knew about and wanted to meet. I didn't know how the exercise would work, but my goal was to get these engineers networking and connecting so that they would improve their personal networking skills but, also, improve the company by sharing ideas that would benefit them.

Again I gave everyone about fifteen minutes to talk. Afterward, I finished my talk and it was time for a late afternoon social hour, complete with great food and drink. I had been asked to purchase 350 copies of our book, *Networlding*. Jocelyn wasn't there. She was busy traveling the world for the company. I had also been asked to sign books for everyone, and so for the next two hours I stood at the front of the room signing one book after another.

During that time, because I had wrapped up my presentation within minutes of that last networking exercise, people had kept networking with the people they had met during the exercises. For the next two hours all I heard were conversations that went something like, "Wow! I didn't know you did that in your department. I think we could benefit by partnering together on purchasing." And "I love what you did addressing that problem with managing new employees in your area. Let's get together and talk further as I would really appreciate getting more input as to what I can do with my team."

In other words, what I was hearing was that people were doing what good networkers do—sharing ideas, support, opportunities, and more connections to yet others who could help in the same way and vice versa.

I had a colleague who had the rare privilege of filming Benjamin Zander, musical director of the Boston Philharmonic Youth Orchestra. She used that film for leadership training. I wish I could have filmed this unique experience. It was life changing for me, and it appeared to be the same for those who attended the event. Sadly, we had not thought of filming, but the experience started me down the path to more and more live events where I got to experiment with the six-degrees concept and see something even more profound—that if you *facilitate networking events you will get better results.*

Over the course of the next decade I would facilitate dozens and dozens of events like the one at Motorola. These included alumni groups from DePaul, Loyola, the University of Chicago, Northwestern, and the Wharton School of Business. I also continued to work with corporations teaching and facilitating networking. And I kept seeing the same results to the reality that … people need help networking and that we need more facilitated networking events, especially now as the online world is actually creating disconnection.

Networking facilitation

What we've discovered from years of running networking events is that facilitators are necessary to help people connect. There are varying statistics about shyness, but we believe it's safe to say that there are a large number of people who consider themselves shy.

Consider Melissa's experience:

> I remember when I was facilitating a networking event on a cruise ship. There was a man named Manny who was brought by his friend, Joe. Manny was okay with Joe sharing with me how shy Manny was with meeting new people, something you can't avoid when it comes to networking. I asked Manny if he would mind if I introduced him at the event and made a special request for people to approach him and *look him in his eyes* when they shook hands with him. He gave me a nod. So when I started my presentation where I gave instructions for our first exercise, I told the audience of over 100 people that Manny was in the group and that he was shy. I requested that they make an

effort to go over to Manny, look him in his eyes and give him a warm welcome.

I didn't think more about this request but after the evening had ended and I was walking out of the room, I heard someone behind me yelling, "Melissa! Melissa! I'm cured! I'm cured!" I turned around to see a very happy Manny with a huge smile plastered all over his face. Those little gestures of connection by the attendees had made all the difference in helping Manny start to appreciate the benefits of facilitated networking.

The point of us telling this story in this chapter is to show how individuals and organizations can create more structured networking events that include trained networking facilitators. This would be a welcome and needed addition to a practice that has been, up until now, too unstructured. If instead, organizations made a point of creating facilitated events that helped people move through the steps of good networking, just think of the progress they would make.

We could see sales departments onboarding their new hires faster, and lawyers, accountants and bankers developing their relationship-building skills to a level where they were much more effective, and, we believe, happier. After all, we are experiencing one of the toughest times in our history when it comes to feeling disconnected.

A growing concern: Adult loneliness

Dr. Oz recently had a segment on the emerging problem of adult loneliness, a problem that is developing into an epidemic due to the growth of social media. Many people are staying home, not going out and meeting others, and opting, instead, to passively watch their lives go by onscreen. Some of the people on the show shared that they were spending up to twelve hours or more on social media sites daily.

Now it may seem odd to add this section into a chapter on the science of networks, but when we see people like Dr. Oz starting a campaign in response to the issue of disconnection because of too much technology, we are seeing evidence of a problem that doesn't look like it is going away any time soon.

When we think about the future of our children, how can we not be concerned about this problem? We've emphasized the importance of live networking. We now want to reiterate the need for organizations to pay attention to this rising issue that will bring with it additional health issues such as depression. Our suggestions for both organizations and individuals include:

- Setting aside time daily to get out and connect with others.
- Finding meetup groups with interests that match yours.
- Exploring events that provide small group exchanges so you can feel less like one of the crowd and more like part of the group.
- Taking time to call people in your network just to tell them you're thinking about them. It's one of the best things you can do to maintain your network.

- Calling organizations that will be beneficial to growing your career and ask them if they have mentorship programs. Here, you can find support from someone who is in your field, someone from whom you can understand some of the isolation issues you might be facing in your particular job.

- Making successful introductions. Melissa points out that the "introduction is the new referral." Why? Because in today's hyper-connected world, we don't often have the time to get to know all those in our network as well as we would like to but we can still connect them and add value to those whom you introduce.

Especially with the rise of home office workers, many of us are at risk of eventually feeling isolated. This is a very real danger. There are many studies published recently that show the many health risks we face because of a lack of social connection. Just remember, it's always ok to reach out and connect—just because. We all need one another. Some of us just show that need more than others. The bottom line here is, don't let your ego get in the way of asking for help.

Tips

- Start with the level of emotional support to open up relationships and create engagement.

- Set up your own structured networking event using the Networlding Support Exchange. Below, Melissa offers her book where you will be able to pull out this section and use it to create great networking exchanges.

- One you host a session, encourage others to do the same. This way all parties involved will start to generate new networking opportunities.

> ***BONUS:** Melissa invites those of you who would like to work through her process to email her at <u>melissa@networlding.com</u>. She will be happy to send a free copy of her full *Networlding Guidebook* in a digital format.

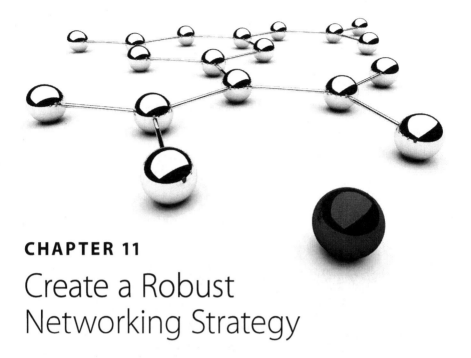

CHAPTER 11

Create a Robust Networking Strategy

Successful people prepare for presentations, speeches, pitches, and meetings all the time. We know that's critical for our success. What most people don't realize though is that being prepared by having a robust networking strategy is just as crucial.

Recently, at the Executive Leadership Council, one of my networks I mentioned earlier, we had twenty-five executives at their headquarters in Charlotte. We were with the CEO of the Teachers Insurance and Annuity Association, Roger Ferguson. We spent the afternoon helping these leaders better understand their business challenges, while giving them insights into Roger's role as CEO and as the board's chairman. He serves on multiple Fortune 1000 boards, so he also offered advice to those interested in being board directors in the future. One of the things that Roger highlighted was having a consistent and deliberate networking strategy.

During the meeting I shared my networking and visibility strategy for getting on a corporate board. First, you can't be seen as going around waving a flag that says, "Pick me, pick me!" But at the same time, you must build your credibility among the members and the leadership. Your strategy involves getting exposure, showing these influencers in your targeted organization how your background and skills are such that you're one of the leaders in your field. Achieving the goal of becoming a desired member means that those influencers must notice you, like what they see as they get to know you, and because you're also good at building rapport on an individual basis, each of them becomes a champion for you inside that group. They start to see you as a potential board director. There are many things you can do to raise your profile.

What does raising your profile entail? It's about writing articles, speaking at conferences, serving on nonprofit boards, getting on board committees, and in general, distinguishing yourself from others. We spent fifteen minutes talking about which nonprofits you should volunteer your time for, and how to stay consistently deliberate and strategic around networking. Search firms may conduct 50 percent of the board searches out there, but the other 50 percent of placements are through networking. Those people already sitting at the board table can recommend you. Or, if there are eleven people on a board and they're looking for that twelfth member, before they go to a search firm, they may say, "Who do we know?" Another question is, "How do you get yourself in that conversation, without promoting yourself?"

If you come across as needy, desperate, or greedy, you're going to have a harder time. People on boards want people who do things fluidly, without overt self-promotion. Again, this is something that speaks to the art of networking. There's a nuance between strategy and manipulation. We've talked about people in the book who fall on one side of that spectrum or the other. In this case, when you're strategically creating connections, your network grows fluidly. The staging of your different networks determines the staging of your career, and how people see you.

Take Biggs Mansion, of which I'm a member. Most Chicagoans refer to as just "Biggs," one of the best cigar clubs in the city. I go to cigar clubs all around the country, but nothing compares to Biggs. First, it's a unique space and experience. Second, if you enjoy cigar smoking, you're there, having a drink, and creating connections with very few distractions. There are ten different rooms, for four to six people, and you're talking about business, family, sports, and hobbies.

I had several friends who were fairly new to cigar smoking, and we shared a glass of scotch and a cigar, and they didn't want to leave. All we did was sit down for three hours and talk. For a networker, it's golden. You're enjoying the environment—the mellow music, the dark leather chairs, the beautiful rooms—and you can actually talk to each other. Whereas when you go to a restaurant, you're leaning in to avoid the distractions.

You feel like you're at home. I have a locker where I keep cigars my friends might need. As a member, I become a host with my own room, my locker, and my handful of guests. If you're not a cigar smoker, I have smaller, flavored cigars that women especially love. I'm increasingly taking potential clients and candidates to Biggs because you can sit down and really talk and make a connection in a very cool environment.

You have one another's full attention. The first floor of Biggs is open to the public, but the second and third floors are for just for members. There are four separate rooms with six chairs each, and there's a back room with pool tables, so you can have a conversation over a game. On the third floor, there are no TVs, just sitting rooms. You sit, smoke, drink, and have conversations. It's become my new go-to spot. The beautiful thing is that out of all my close friends, none are members. So this much more social network of mine allows me to share unique experiences with them, and also build new connections successfully.

Biggs gives me an opportunity to have a real conversation and to get people's energy in a unique place. But I can also meet one-on-one, which I've done many times. Often someone will mention grabbing a drink or a bite, and I'll suggest Biggs. You can order from nearby restaurants, and the servers deliver to your sitting room. One of the most interesting times was when I invited three people, none of whom knew each other. They all arrived separately, and I was there in advance to secure a room with four chairs. Two on one side, two on the other, all of us facing one another across a table. I know all three, so I knew what they like to drink—I've already got it in my locker—and it's relaxing. They're interested in learning about one another, so we tell stories about how we met. After three hours, we're exchanging business cards. I arranged it that way because each of them wanted to catch up with me, but I knew they would also be interested in meeting each other.

As a result of this experience, everyone benefitted. They all exchanged cards, and I sent them all an email to connect them—"Thanks for joining me last week at Biggs. I had a great time. I hope you guys can connect"—and everyone responded. All three received either friendship or business out of the meeting—a win-win!

One-on-one vs. group networking

In a one-on-one meeting versus a connecting-people meeting there are a few things I consider. What level of connection exists already? If there's not a strong connection already, I'm hesitant to bring other people into that. I want to build my one-on-one connections first.

That's why I belong to social clubs like Biggs, the Metropolitan Club, Ruffled Feathers (the golf club by my house), and Club Corp. I don't think I enjoy any of the other clubs as much as Biggs—and not because I smoke many cigars. I enjoy it there because you make unbelievable connections. People aren't there randomly. I've invited my guests into a social, face-to-face environment. We take our time connecting, sharing stories and creating strong bonds. The environment inspires networking. They're there to socialize and smoke cigars. They're the people you invite, and that you spend time connecting with.

Tips

- **Consider where you're currently networking.** Is there a special go-to place you have where everybody knows your name, (like Cheers)?

- **Remember to look for a quiet place where you can hear the other person.** If you have to raise your voice to talk, your conversation and connection may be compromised. Just suggest, "Why don't we step over here to a quieter spot where we can hear one another better?"

- **You have only one chance to make a first winning impression.** Make sure you have set yourself up for success with the space you choose to start and build great connections.

Developing a networking plan and timeline

Probably the best way to illustrate the concept of creating a networking plan with a timeline integrated into it is to give you an example. Every two years, Chicago United runs a business leadership conference. They identify forty-five minority business leaders—black, Hispanic, Asian—according to certain criteria. Candidates are nominated, complete an application, and then a review is conducted.

In 2003, they nominated the first class, and among those leaders was a young community organizer named Barack Obama. Michelle Obama represented the 2005 class. I was nominated in 2007, but I wasn't selected that time. I was disappointed because it's a big honor in Chicago. From then on, I set a goal to become a business leader of color. I didn't know Gloria, Chicago United's Executive Director, at the time, so I asked my friend, Roger Crockett, whom I mentioned before, to introduce me to her. However, it wasn't until 2009 that I was nominated and selected as a "business leader of color."

It's a prominent list of people. In 2009, several partners, including Kevin, the CEO, at the time, of my company Heidrick & Struggles, nominated me. Before the big gala in November, they always bring the past business leaders of color to welcome the new class. What's significant is that one of the people I nominated was Roger, the person who had introduced me to Gloria. Roger was one of fifty people selected to be a business leader of color in 2015, so it all came full circle. And at least two other people whom I nominated were inducted.

What's even more amazing? I agreed to host and chair of the selection committee. Consider that in 2006, I didn't even make the list. Then in 2009, I made the list, and now here I am—the one *making* the list. I'm the speaker and host, and I'm welcoming all forty-five people into the Chicago United Business Leaders of Color. It's an incredible feeling and another full circle moment.

I'm glad that I understand the span of years now. That's why the timeline is great, to realize we were connected through a friend, who worked for Jocelyn Carter-Miller, Melissa's co-author of *Networlding*, whom we mentioned earlier. Now, nine years later, Melissa and I are writing this book together, just as she and Jocelyn had done back in 2000. Our long timeline shows you have to be patient. When you take the time to start by creating great connections with quality people, over time, your achieve an a progression of additional great connections. Time leverages the strength and dept of your network.

So, as I was waiting to speak, reviewing the speech in my head, I kept thinking, "This is crazy." Up until that moment, I hadn't reflected on what had transpired. I remembered how I was initially rejected, but now I was chairing the Chicago United Selection Committee and inducting one of my friends..

When I got turned down, I didn't take it as an offense—I wanted to meet Gloria Castillo who was at the helm of this organization. Between 2007 and 2015, I was consistent in supporting and giving back to Chicago United. I provided ideas, I recommended giving Gloria an honorary membership at the Metropolitan Club, I encouraged Heidrick to become a supporting member, and I nominated two of my partners as business leaders of color.

There was a definite, consistent track record of work, giving back, and earning respect. Gloria is one of the few people who knows the full story, because I told her about my personal journey. Recently, I told her that the university president at Saginaw Valley just asked me to be their commencement speaker. It's crazy, but I am so humbled by the networks and how the benefits of nurturing them come back to you over time.

Local vs. national

We talk a lot about Chicago United. I view them as a local networking group that boasts unbelievable connections with some of the major companies in the Chicago area and that connects people in many industries. The goal of identifying business leaders of color is to identify people who could serve on corporate boards. I like to feel that I've played a part by not only being recognized myself, but also in helping them fine-tune that goal. I helped create an executive speakers series at the Metropolitan Club, a deliberate local strategy to create a platform to have business and though leaders interact with members of the club.

Formal networks

The formal network I spend the most time with is the Executive Leadership Council (ELC), my corporate board initiative. It was for them that I participated in the Charlotte meeting with the executives at TIAA-CREF. I followed up by sending an email to the Corporate Board Initiative, to inform them I had a conversation with the team at Twitter. As a result they hosted an event ELC and Heidrick & Struggles at their offices in San Francisco in February. Those types of networks go way beyond our local Chicago connection.

What's interesting about this Twitter collaboration is that one of my contacts, Monica Pool Knox, was in HR there at the time. I advised her when she was looking for a job. We've known each other for twenty years. She was now at the level where I could recommend her for the ELC, so I did and she was approved to join. She was so grateful, she asked if there was anything she could do for me. This was how the Twitter event was set up. She is now an ELC member. That's an example of a win-win. Monica is now with Microsoft and I look forward to more ways I can support her growth and success.

Short-term vs. long-term strategies

How do you consider the timeframe for your strategies? Sometimes, when we look at the payoff for developing a connection, or looking to network, people are shortsighted. They're transactional, in the moment, looking for a job, a promotion, or *something*. On the contrary, I always look at the long-term play, with potential for short-term milestones. With Monica, for example—that relationship has lasted twenty years. She started at GTE, and I've supported her along the way in looking for her next move. Getting her into ELC wasn't about getting Twitter to host an event for us—it was about her. But she happened to be at a company in an industry that ELC wants to be represented in. The suggestion for a meeting just popped up. She was excited to help me after feeling that I helped her for so long. It is a great friendship but around helping those people in our network and by helping those who helps us.

That's what I'm getting at—people often want the payoff to be immediate, but the long-term relationship can be so much richer.

One of the goals I work toward daily is being "awake in my network," the realization that as we move in and out of networks daily we build an ability to see connections and possible opportunities and say, "Wow, I should go have a talk with those people in my network who are in my inner circle."

Most people don't explore their networks this way, but this is our daily world. I think that stems from the basic philosophy of always looking to network to give. Because then you can give more, and as a result, make more happen for you and others. And with Monica, I could see potential, expanding opportunities for both of us, because we both have become skilled at staying awake in our networks.

And the connection is not for the immediate payoff—it's long-term. We've talked about everything under the sun, both personally and professionally. There's a connection. There's a friendship. When I told Monica I would introduce her to another friend of mine in HR at Google when I'm in San Francisco, she said, "Oh, Billy, you're always looking out for me." Of course I am!

That's the thing about connecting—in your long-term strategy, connecting plays a huge strategic role. It goes full-circle. You can constantly build on it. What if more people, in this long-term conversation, would start thinking of this as building blocks? What if more people saw connecting other people as building their own network? It's always at the top of my mind—who else could they network with?

In many cases, they have some of these relationships already. That reminds me of something I said to a buddy once on a golf trip twenty years ago. There were ten of us, and we'd taken a trip together before. It was the third day on a four-day trip. We golfed, then we had a steak dinner with drinks and a cigar. We were enjoying each other's company.

Everybody was moving in the direction of settling down. I said, "This group here, we're going to be friends for the rest of our lives. We're all at similar stages in our lives. And this is very different from the people we went to high school with. At that time we were all in our early thirties, and had either just gotten married or were already married and starting to have children.

"All of these things that we're going through, we're going to be connected by." Sure enough, twenty years later, we still are. And what connected us was because we were going through these life experiences together. That was our commonality. I attended all their weddings and hope to attend their children's weddings too! I made that statement not considering the implications—but twenty years later, it's still true.

Tips

- **Allow serendipities to happen.** People may come into your life for a reason, a season, or a lifetime, but you don't strategically say, "I'm going to go out and look for this person."

- **Look at your career in three-year increments.** That enables you to stay focused. You don't want to stay too comfortable. Decide whether you want to stay on for another three years or move on. Set goals to accomplish during that time.

- **Throw yourself a challenge.** Say you're good at marketing and sales. Explore building your technology skills.

- **Get visible.** Sit on a panel or volunteer for an in-house project that's not part of your daily workload, or join a nonprofit.

- Be helpful. Always think about how you can help others with building their networks.

Your target list

Initially, you only need one networking partner in your primary circle. In an extensive study Melissa and her team conducted by interviewing two hundred executives, they discovered that the majority of people connect with only five-to-ten networking partners monthly. This means that even one person with whom you share similar or complementary values and who is ready, willing and able to become a networking partner, can create a whole new world of opportunities for you and you for them.

Again, don't think about quantity, but quality. Be selective.

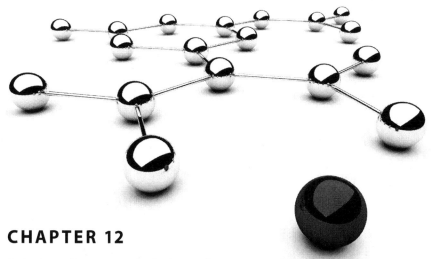

CHAPTER 12

Use Social Media to Create Connections that Matter

I spend 80 percent of my time networking face-to-face. But social media and online networking are very important. Social media enables us to stay in contact more easily, and even make contact more easily. How do you follow up after making a connection? How do you stay in touch? Social media has created an unprecedented opportunity to keep the glue together in your networks. Some people use it better than others.

Melissa has been at the forefront of the online networking curve, having worked as a consultant with a company named Six Figure Jobs, where she helped executives in transition get new jobs. We've both been creating networks for over twenty-five years, and obviously that was well before social media and even before the widespread use of the internet. What's interesting is that we both see that after all these technological advances, fundamentally, it's still all about creating connections that matter.

High tech and high touch

Facebook, LinkedIn, and Twitter are all tools to help us connect better. At the core, social media is a networking tool. But it's *not* a network. I can use social media in addition to a phone call, a meeting, or an email. It's an instantaneous way of contacting someone. I can share a photo or an article, and I can connect you with someone else. When I'm figuring out how I can be helpful, social media can be a powerful tool.

Sometimes it's uncanny how my connections can keep tabs on what I'm doing. I won't have mentioned an event or an award, but they'll have seen it online. It's also interesting now when I talk to people during our introductory thirty-minute conversations, the other person is coming to me well-prepared. They have a good overview of me and my experience from their online research. It's social proof for them, and the thirty minutes are so much richer because some preliminaries are already known.

Branch out

When you start building your network, you're using a lens. The lens I lean on the most is "diversity." I'm always looking through that lens, but unfortunately it's not what other people are commonly looking for. Some people stay in their own neighborhoods and never go downtown. But there's more diversity in major cities than in the suburbs, which are more homogenous.

The same is true for people on social media, where the majority of people connect with people they already know or people who are quite similar to them. They don't extend externally. How can people extend beyond the groups of people they already know?

Seek out new connections on Facebook or LinkedIn who might be in your same industry or social circles, but who have different backgrounds and life experiences from yours.

Helping your net *work* with LinkedIn

LinkedIn is the most business-focused and powerful social media platform for finding job opportunities, attracting qualified candidates for jobs you're seeking to fill, expanding your influence, and, of course, growing your network. Those who use it halfheartedly are missing out on a potential goldmine of leads, valuable contacts, and ear-to-the-ground information about what's happening in their industry.

Like all social media platforms, you want to establish trust with others in your network. That means being aware that what you say about yourself must be true and not exaggerated. Ask current and former colleagues to recommend you for particular skills and reciprocate by doing the same for them.

Start with your profile

Make sure your photograph is up to date, in focus, and as professional as possible. Don't add extraneous details from the background; crop in tight so your smiling face is all the viewer sees.

Be sure your professional headline accurately describes your role. Some examples LinkedIn offers include Experienced Transportation Executive, Web Designer and Information Architect, or Visionary Entrepreneur and Investor. Keep in mind that you have only a few seconds to grab a viewer's attention, so be succinct and not too clever.

LinkedIn will prompt you to keep adding to your profile until you reach "all-star status." You'll want to include the schools you attended, including high school, college, and any other studies. Also, be sure to add your interests and hobbies. Whether it's gourmet cooking or cigar smoking, golf or NASCAR racing, letting people know about what you like to do in your spare time will help others with similar interests find and connect with you. The more you share about yourself, the more people will trust you.

Ask to connect

Once you tell LinkedIn where you've worked and gone to school, the site will recommend people you might want to connect with. As we've discussed throughout this book, the *quality* of your connections is much more than the *quantity*. Only connect with people you actually know, or have met, or would like to meet.

Use InMail

Even with a free account you can message particular contacts through the site. You might use this feature to ask someone to introduce you to a person they know, tell them you're looking for employment, our just to reach out and say hello.

Consider upgrading your account

If you find yourself drawn to LinkedIn as a way to expand and make use of your network, you might want to purchase a premium subscription. There are four different premium plans:

Career. LinkedIn claims that candidates with a Premium Career account get hired an average of two times faster than others. This plan lets you direct message recruiters or job posters through InMail, see who's viewed your profile and how they found you, become a featured applicant and move to the top of recruiters' applicant lists, and even compare yourself to other candidates. You also get access to online video courses via LinkedIn Learning.

Business Plus. With this plan you get fifteen InMail messages per month that let you contact anyone, even if you're not connected. You can see who's viewed your profile and how they found you. You'll also find business insights into a company's growth and trends, and you'll get unlimited people browsing from search results and suggested profiles, as well as access to online video courses.

Sales Navigator Professional. If you're a salesperson, this is the plan for you. You get twenty InMail messages, and you can see who's viewed your profile and get insights into your accounts and leads such as job changes, company growth, and more. This plan also includes unlimited people browsing, and lets you build custom lead lists with advanced search filters to help you zero in on decision-makers. You'll also get lead recommendations, and you can save leads to stay up to date.

Take a course on how to use LinkedIn

There are numerous online courses you can take to learn how to get the most from LinkedIn, some free, and others requiring payment.

Engage with your community

You can also use LinkedIn to post articles and insights about your industry to people in your network. If you're the author, you can become known as an expert, and even if all you do is forward interesting links you come across, people begin to think of you as someone who is engaged and influential.

Tests and certifications

The site also offers links to particular tests and courses that you can take to enhance your skills and verify your competence. You can take a trial course free for the first month, and the topics are targeted to your particular industry and interests.

Stay active

Like any social media site, your contacts will lose interest if you're not actively posting over time. They also won't like it if they send you an InMail and you don't see it or answer it for two weeks. Check in every day if possible, or every other day if that's too much.

Helping your net *work* with Facebook

Most of us remember life before Facebook. Now it seems like everyone is spending hours a day posting pictures of their children, projects, political views, and more. Facebook is so pervasive that we seldom give it much thought. That's really unfortunate, because if you share ideas and photos on Facebook without considering who will read your posts and how they might react to them, you can quickly damage your personal brand. I always like to think of how a particular post might be viewed by my mother.

Be conscious

Building the right image on Facebook takes a lot strategic planning. You have to think about what might be interesting to your network. Your Facebook network is nothing like the business focus found on LinkedIn. It includes everyone from your 80-year-old aunt to your ex-girlfriend or boyfriend, your siblings, their friends, your cousins, in-laws, people you used to or currently work with, potential clients and future employers, former teachers or classmates—you get the picture.

With such a wide range of people seeing your posts, you have to be careful what you say and do. Like all networking you do, you want to build trust, and strengthen your brand. Be careful about alienating others by expressing strident political or religious views. Don't mindlessly forward some bit of news or a made-up claim that comes your way unless you do a little research and make sure it's not a rumor or falsehood. Remember, everything you post can be seen by almost anyone, and will be online virtually forever.

Don't brag

Many times, it seems like people post things to Facebook only to make themselves look good. Nobody likes a show-off. People prefer self-deprecating humor, unusual occurrences, lovely photos, or pithy observations over seeing your shiny new car or ostentatious house. They like seeing pictures of you with your family and friends, and can tolerate photos of your Hawaiian vacation if they aren't meant as a way to show off.

Look for how you can serve

Rather than use Facebook to make yourself look better, use it to gain insight into others' lives. When you find out someone's parent just died, or their child went off to college, consider what they might need from you. Likewise, if they've moved to a new city, reach out to them and ask them what they like or dislike about it. Did someone get laid off? Send a message letting them know you're thinking about them, and tell them you'll keep your eye out for opportunities. Does this way of networking sound familiar? It should; all through this book we've been talking about looking first for ways you can give *to* your connections rather than what you can get *from* them.

Discover what your connections care about

If you're meeting a new prospect for lunch, see if you can find out more about them by studying their Facebook page. You'll discover if they have a family, what kinds of challenges they face in their daily life, maybe where they went to school or grew up, and much more. You can use this information to create a bond with someone. "I came across the photo of your daughter's ballet recital. My daughter took ballet for ten years." But be careful sharing too much of what you've found out: people don't want to feel like you've been stalking them.

Engage

Don't just read other people's posts; react to them. Like, comment on, or share posts that speak to you. Try not to get into arguments when you disagree; keep things civil. Remember, when you like or share someone else's post, you're tacitly agreeing with it, and that might have implications for some of your online friends.

Join groups

Groups are one of the most powerful ways you can engage a network on Facebook. There are dozens of different categories, including Local, Friends, Games, Buy and Sell, Funny, Identity & Relationships, Spiritual & Inspirational, Food, Sports, Cars & Motorcycles, Health & Fitness, News & Politics, Arts & Culture, Animals & Pets, Home & Garden, Support & Comfort, Style, Parenting, Travel & Places, Science & Tech, Professional Networking, Outdoor Activities, Neighborhood & Community, Photography, Business, School & Education, Hobby & Leisure, and Trending.

With all those categories, you should be able to find a group or two that interests you. But it's more powerful for building your network if you're able to meet your new Facebook friends face-to-face and in the flesh. That's where the category "Local" comes in. By exploring the groups in your community, you'll find people you can engage with in person—always more powerful than a simple online connection.

Helping your net *work* with Twitter

Twitter is the real-time social media platform. Think of it as a starting point for building a network.

Decide what you want to talk about

If you're intending to use Twitter to build your network, you need a focus. If you talk about everything that pops into your head, people might not want to follow you. On the other hand, if you stick to one or two subjects, your followers will start to see you as a source of inside information on those topics.

Create a strong profile

Just like LinkedIn, your profile page is important on Twitter. It gives people an understanding of who you are and what you're about with just a quick glance. Be sure it's up-to-date and compelling.

Follow people you want to get to know

If there's someone you'd like to get to know, follow them and retweet their tweets. Use their Twitter handles (@marksmith) to send messages directly to them.

Use it to go local

Twitter is a great way to arrange local events. #Chicago or #Miami in a tweet can help assemble a small group to meet for drinks to discuss a neighborhood issue, or a large crowd to welcome home a local hero. It's a good way to promote local events and happenings too.

Helping your net *work* with emails and texts

OK, maybe email and text messaging aren't exactly social media, but they can be valuable tools when it comes to building and maintaining your network. Send a text to a connection on a day you know they might be facing a difficult situation. It lets them know you're thinking about them and wishing them well. If you take an interesting photo, send it to one or more of your connections and ask them what they think. It's more personal to receive a photo that was sent specifically to you on your mobile phone than to come across it in a Facebook post.

A weekly or monthly email newsletter sent to a select group of your network connections can keep you top of mind. Just be sure it contains valuable information that people can use and will welcome reading.

As we said at the beginning of this chapter, social media can be a very powerful tool for building your network. But don't come to depend on it totally, because it doesn't replace the day-to-day value of personal networking and the human touch.

Also note that although online connecting continues to increase, according to research by Forbes, "more than 8 out of 10 said they prefer in-person, face-to-face meetings to technology-enabled ones." Therefore, whenever possible, request in-person meetings, at least at the start of building a relationship.

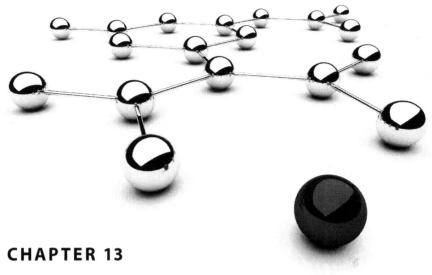

CHAPTER 13
Become a Network Thinker

Networking is borderless. It has no walls, but many doors. Having spent a lot of time on college campuses, I know that our experiences are captured in a space. There are people who come into that space, and you have common experiences with them—both inside and outside the classroom. Eventually, you're stamped as a graduate of the university with its walls and borders. There are other universities, other institutions, but they're all built around a similar concept. The differences are the people, a few classes, and the location, but they're generally the same.

My lens says "diversity first." I look to create a collaborative, mutually beneficial atmosphere that occurs best when you create a diverse network. You can do this best by continuously making a commitment to building connections with diverse people.

Top performance is the end game. If you can do well in the world, and do very well financially, that's even better than only doing the latter. Top performance is also expected in top organizations. If you're going to have top performance, it's better to have sustainable top performance than top performance that peaks and troughs across quarters.

The other lens I turn to all the time is sincerity and giving. It encompasses all the other lenses. It's always about the people. It's always about the relationships. Trust yourself in order to go the distance.

What's interesting is that all of those friendships started *after* I moved to Chicago. I'm probably only connected to four or five guys that I went to college with. But my close friends all stem from my Chicago days when I had to reinvent myself because I was scared to death.

If you fail to build significant relationships, you'll likely have regrets. You don't want regret in your life. I'm naturally outgoing, but I know I need to constantly work at building relationships. I'm happy to be the one to make the first move because I know that first step is all about helping the other person. Knowing that this is my foundation, I don't wait to make a connection.

I reference again that first time I read George C. Fraser's book, *Success Runs in Our Race.*" He was the first writer on networking I was exposed to. As I was reading I remember reading and thinking, "This is what I do! He wrote it down exactly how it is." One of my most fascinating networking connections happened six months later, when I had the opportunity to sit across the table from George. At that time I had created networking receptions around the country with Savoy magazine. They were called i2i Networking. My thought was, "How can we make this different? Let's bring in George Fraser." To be able to make a call to the thought leader who'd given me clarity to introduce myself, and then have the resources to bring him in—it was a revelation.

Connecting and growing a network is an incredible feeling and a skill that we all should cultivate. But to be part of a network that you've created yourself, that wouldn't exist without you, like my golf circle—that's another feeling entirely. Crafting a network takes strategy, collaboration, and creation of an entity that can sustain itself. I put in the original legwork to build the connections with my golf buddies, and I brought all of us together. But now it's a self-sustaining group. Whenever we're in our respective cities, no matter how many of us are there, we make an effort to connect with one another. Sometimes it's quick—a drink, a round of golf on a long weekend, or a cup of coffee. Our network sustains itself now, and that's the end goal.

As Mahatma Gandhi stated, "Your beliefs become your thoughts, Your thoughts become your words, Your words become your actions, Your actions become your habits, Your habits become your values, Your values become your destiny." It all starts with what you think. That's why we have spent so much time sharing with you how Melissa and I challenged ourselves to think differently about networking, to think in a way that would create the best results for those in our networks.

Bringing it home

The whole idea behind being a network thinker is that you're always thinking about how you can connect others, add value, and help those who need help. This is something that you need to develop and then integrate into your lifestyle. By that, we mean that the process becomes such a part of you that you can't turn it off, even if you want to. Connecting people became part of who Melissa and I are because it was what we both needed to do to survive all those years ago when I struggled in college and Melissa struggled significantly in her early years as an entrepreneur.

I went from an all-black neighborhood with few college-educated people to a preppy, predominantly white college. I was painfully aware of how much I didn't fit in. I lacked study skills. I had no network. But through it all, I didn't stop to think what it would be like when suddenly I was there at Saginaw Valley, completely unprepared for my first day.

I recall the first day of classes, specifically Psychology 101. There were sixty-five students in my class, and I was the only black person. The professor explained the bell curve: no matter what, a certain percentage will fail. The bottom line was that 20 percent of us weren't going to make it.

At the time I thought, "How does he know I'm not going to make it? He doesn't even know me!" I'd already put myself in that failure category before the lecture really even started. Then the professor started lecturing and everybody took notes. It was then I realized that

I'd never taken notes before. I didn't know how to be a college student and this was the first day of the next four years of my life.

On days two and three, the same thing happened: an hour in class, everyone took notes, people asked questions, and I tried to hide so he wouldn't call on me. By Friday that first week, it hit me: I was in over my head. College was a dream, but I was getting nothing out of it. I had no idea about any of the resources that the school had set up for people like me. Until then, everything had been on me: applying for college, getting accepted, and picking classes. I thought I had total responsibility, and I didn't even realize anyone would even *want* to help me.

It wasn't until I went back to my college as an adult--as a successful executive receiving the distinguished alumni award--that I realized how the help I received there had such a big impact on my life. I was on campus to receive the award, being given a tour with an entourage—Gisel, my wife, the provost, student leaders—and they showed me how the campus had evolved over the past twenty-seven years. As we walked past the lecture hall where I had those tutoring sessions, I became emotional. I peeked in and saw no one was there, so I asked all seven people in the tour to come in. They sat down in the front row and I told my story for the first time ever. Looking back, I see now that my tutor and my friend Mike, were sent by got to help me get a good start in my career. I couldn't tell you my tutor's name. I don't remember what he looked like, but he was enthusiastic about tutoring me, and his enthusiasm changed my life.

I started thinking about the different ways my tutor got me to study. This part of my story is especially emotional for me—something I hadn't looked back on in twenty-seven years. I never realized how crucial it was until I started telling my story, and noticed these little things that happened along the way are things that have actually made big differences in my life. There had been little hiccups that could have changed my life. Any left or right turn off of my path could have taken me in an entirely different direction. At the time, I just knew to stick to my promise to myself: "I'm not going back to Detroit without a degree.." But the message from God, I believe was, "Stay on your path. I got you."

I've come to embrace my experience as a message I would like to pass on to others: "You can get there from here." This means that no matter where you started or are currently starting, you can get where you want to go. It's really up to you. There's a path, and you can get there. You can make powerful requests. You can pray, but it really comes down to you in the end. By sharing this moment from my past, I was connecting with those student leaders and the tour group, to the power of networking to help others. My friend, Mike, didn't have to stop to talk with me on that day so long ago. He didn't have to connect with me, or listen to my story, or meet with or help me. But he did. You can't turn true and caring networking on and off. Further, if you commit to the practice of this type of networking, it becomes part of your character, how you act, who you are. It's your life.

Tips

- Network thinking is about being aware of both whom you network with and how you network.

- Think about your current network. Surprisingly, most people don't take the time to do this. It also helps to do this daily if possible. Write down the names of the top five people you have in your network who have either introduced you to someone or a number of people or referred you or have even taken time to talk to you about your career goals.

- Take your list and email, one at a time, each person sharing with them that you would like to get together with them and find out how you might be of support with their career goals. If you have been the one introducing, referring or giving to your network, you can say something like this that Melissa has found success with, "Hi X. It's been some time since we last spoke. I'd like to get together with you for coffee or a lunch to catch up and explore ways we can help one another."

- Attend networking events with the question, "Who is the person in your network you admire most?" Then ask them why. These questions will help you locate people who are network thinkers and therefore helping you and them consciously build stronger and more sustainable networks.

- Expand your network thinking by looking for values-based leaders.

- Author Richard Barrett is an internationally recognized thought leader on the evolution of human values in business and society. He is the founder and chairman of the Barrett Values Centre®, a Fellow of the World Business Academy and Former Values Coordinator at the World Bank. He shares the following about values-based leaders: They have a holistic perspective on life. They can handle multiple levels of complexity. They are focused on the questions, 'How can I help?' and 'What can I do?' They are concerned about the state of the world and social justice. They also care about the legacy they are leaving for future generations." Take time daily, if possible, to search for these connections. They will be eager to hear form you if your values match up.

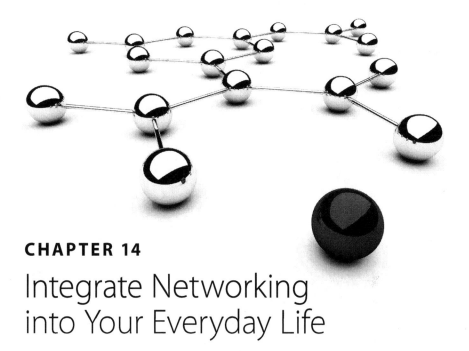

CHAPTER 14

Integrate Networking into Your Everyday Life

When I think about all the things I've written about networking so far—network to give, not to get; be a network thinker; make real connections—all of these things are important. But a final thing that has made my net *work* is something that outsiders have constantly remarked about: understanding the awareness that you walk in and out of networks every day. As I mentioned earlier, Melissa and I call it being *awake in your network*. In other words, if you're vigilant, you'll see regular opportunities to make connections that create opportunities for yourself and others while, simultaneously, continuing to grow the strength of your network. Just as the people who buy from you most will be repeat buyers, those who refer opportunities to you will refer again.

I travel for my job, and, like many professionals, have family commitments that include taking care of my two children after working ten to twelve hours a day. With frequent travel, things get complex and challenging. From the outside, many people have commented on my ability to be a master networker with all of my other commitments. However, it's less about the time required and more about my philosophy behind this commitment. It's about making the initial effort to integrate networking into your lifestyle.

Every item on my calendar and every decision I make about networking is strategic and intentional. The networks where I invest my time are those I'm passionate about and have interests that I can share with my friends and family.

Ultimately, over time, my time becomes a network of connected events, organizations, and people, all of which I walk in and out of every day. Because I've interconnected my networks there are days when I can touch five or six of them, whether by phone, online, or at events. My interconnected networks have also enabled me to sit on six boards. It's the power of *integrating* your networks that will generate the most benefits daily for you too.

One of the networks I've mentioned before is the Executive Leadership Council (ELC), representing a key part of my networking lifestyle. Why? Because it's a national organization that connects six hundred or so of the most senior corporate executives in the country. Here, I'm on the board of directors and a co-chair on their Corporate Board Initiative. I created the Corporate Board Initiative to try to find a way to give back to the ELC. Their membership comprises professional colleagues who help me with my job as I help them, a very powerful *exchange*.

The ELC wanted to create a way to prepare their members for board membership, and that's what Heidrick does. I immersed myself in helping them and by doing so I get so much back in return.

Getting to that next level of networking, whether it's getting an introduction or meeting, or being invited to join a club or organization, or becoming a board member, takes a certain amount of strategy. It requires you to look at the landscape of your potential connections and assess where you are and where you want to be connected. Then connect your networking into your lifestyle.

Take the Goodman Theatre, for example, another one of my connection hubs. My wife and I enjoy going to their shows. We're season ticket holders, and as we've gone to shows over the years, we've met a variety of people on their board. Over time, I heard about a business group at the theater. I started asking questions about it and discovered that fifty companies in Chicago are represented on the council. It turned out that over half of the people from those companies are Heidrick clients or people from companies with whom we're interested in developing relationships. I thought being on this business council would be a good way to develop relationships that might eventually lead to business for Heidrick—and at the same time, I can enjoy the theater! We have entertained many clients that eventually gave us work and made connections by enjoying the theater.

Additionally, we got connected to one of the premier cultural institutions in Chicago. Heidrick realized this was a win-win, and I wondered why they hadn't considered this before.

We signed up and Heidrick wanted me to represent them. I hadn't approached them intending to be their representative, but of course I wanted it, theater buff that I am, so I accepted. Now we develop great relationships with our clients and partners at these theater events.

After two years, the Goodman asked me to lead their business council. Again, my goal was exposure to fifty companies. That year, one of the featured events was a performance of a famed play by August Wilson. At the start of each season, they give the business council a preview of the year's upcoming performances. They had a series they wanted to do around August Wilson.

I left the meeting considering several ideas because I love Wilson's work. The end result was that I asked the Met Club if they would hold a reception to hear about upcoming events at the Goodman in relation to Wilson's work, *and* we'd have actors do a preview of the play. The Met Club was all over it. They covered the cost of food and drink in exchange for the opportunity to get potential new members into the club. The Goodman became connected to people in my network who may or may not know their theater, but know the playwright, and the Goodman promoted their upcoming season. Both organizations loved the idea, ironed out the details, and over one hundred people attended. I represented both boards and introduced the play with the executive director of the theater, Maria Castro. I created an event with people from three groups: my own network, the Metropolitan Club, and the Goodman. All of this resulted in three wins from one event.

You can create the same interconnected synergies and, as a result, more effectively leverage your networks. It starts with creating one significant relationship and then another, and then continuing, one connection at a time, to make introductions and offer support to those connections. This is giving on your part that will build stronger relationships. Then, as you combine your one-to-one networking to include participating and supporting other networks that can become connection hubs (like professional associations or social clubs), you'll see the benefits of your efforts.

Maintaining your network

Maintaining your network involves checking in with your networking partners at least once a month. I call this "massaging your network" because it conjures up the physical idea of touching, working through muscles and joints, and making a connection. A massage doesn't happen without a touch. A network doesn't happen without a connection.

Many groups I'm involved in help me maintain my networks. For example, I'll receive tickets from the Goodman board that I can give away to potential clients or those in my network. For me, that's a touch point.

Sometimes it's an email, a call, or a cigar, but often I'll send a note saying I'm thinking about the person. It's simply staying in touch. When you do that, you'll find that when you need that person, or vice versa, even though it's been a long time, it's much easier to reconnect.

Take one of my good friends, Steve Pemberton, the chief diversity officer for Walgreens. We don't get the chance to spend a lot of time in person, but we have many touch points. And they're respected touch points. Because we have regular touch points, I'm happy to make a connection. Often, he'll connect me with a person in his network that he'd like me to spend time with, and that invariably results in a valuable connection. I'll share an insight and that person will share his or her story. It happened again recently with a friend of his, and she later told Steve how valuable a connection I turned out to be for her. He wrote me saying, "She loved talking to you. She thought you were extremely helpful. I just wanted to say I appreciate you for making the time." That feedback loop is self-sustaining. It's a good strategy for staying in touch.

Another friend of mine also has regular touch points with me. He reached out to me recently and said, "Hey, Billy, I know we haven't been in touch for a while, but I've got some people chasing me for an opportunity they'd like me to consider. I would really appreciate your insight into this, because I'm not sure if it's the right thing. But I know I would get the right advice from you, if you have thirty minutes for me to run this idea by you." I had many things going on, but because of our touch points along the way, I made time for him. I told him I'd talk in the car on my way home at 8:30 or 9:00 p.m. I wouldn't do that for just anyone. Connections like this happen because we stayed in touch.

These are intentional moments that I don't leave to chance. If there's someone in my network whom I haven't talked to in some time, I'll send a note for any reason—downtime or a chance reminder—to stay in touch. Even a simple text that says, "Hey, what's going on? I haven't seen you in a while." I sent just such a text to someone I used to work with who sees me as a mentor. I was waiting for an appointment, thought of him by chance, and shot him the text. He responded saying, "Man! I was just thinking about you. Let's connect again." That happens a great deal, because I'm making those deliberate points of contact often. It's not serendipity if you do it enough.

Get back to those with whom you network. Take the initiative to follow up. Keep in touch. There are countless times where I've done that, touching base by happenstance when the opportunity comes up. Much of what I've written circles back to one key point: being deliberate and intentional. You must trust yourself, too, because then you'll always be comfortable reaching out. Be open to adding value and to giving. Trust that you have something to offer. That's a big chasm for some people when networking, especially young people. Once you integrate the principles of networking into your life, it becomes easier and less time consuming.

I know not everyone works at a company willing to spend $15,000 on a table or a board membership. But you can start small. Connect one of your networks to another. You can start with just bringing two, like-valued people or organizations together as Melissa advocates.

If you're looking at creating and sustaining vibrant networks, you have to truly understand the value equation. When you do that, you can merge networking into your life and create a seamless integration. But if you're out there doing ad-hoc networking, thinking something like, "maybe I'll go there and try that"—which is the way many people network incorrectly—you won't reach sustainability. That's where the big value and payoff is. It's not about the number of people in your network. Remember, as we said earlier, it's about the *quality*.

Tips

- **Take time to pause.** Step away from your everyday routine and reflect on your connections. Think about things like who you currently know who might be good people to introduce them to or resources that might benefit them. This time will help you build even deeper, long-lasting relationships while increasing a spirit of reciprocity to offer similar support to you.

- **Create a networking plan, then work it.** Keep going back to your plan to adapt it to the results you're getting. Include your strategies for networlding into your marketing plan. As you become more accurate at projecting, you'll build skills in visualizing and implementing. Integrate a social media strategy calendar in your plan so you continue to expand your presence on the web.

- **Set realistic goals.** If your goals are not realistic, they're just dreams, not goals. They should be aggressive enough for you to feel a sense of accomplishment by achieving them, but not unrealistic. A goal should be a challenge, not a chore.

- **Create small networking events.** It may be 4-6 people over dinner, movie, concert. Find unique ways to connect.

- **Become a resource for others.** A technique for gaining visibility and credibility is to write or email editors of periodicals.

Contact reporters who write about your field and offer yourself as a resource for additional articles. Whatever you can do to make a reporter's job easier is usually greatly appreciated.

- **Follow up and follow through.** Follow up, if you can, within 24 hours of a meeting, to summarize your conversation for the person you were networking with. This might look something like this: "Billy, you said you were going to introduce me to Susan. I said I was going to introduce you to Derrick. Here is Derrick's information. In my next email I will make an introduction per your request. In the meantime, I look forward to getting introduced to Susan."

- **Focus on your connections and how you can help them.** You only need a few people with whom you're growing deeper professional relationships to focus on monthly. In fact, the average executive has only about five people he or she keeps in regular contact with monthly. Therefore, spend more time thinking about supporting fewer people. This attention will help your leverage the power of your network to, in turn, respond to your needs as one of their select few.

- **Share your knowledge.** Offer those in your network a preview of your skills and talents. They'll then be able to use what you have to offer in exchange for support you're seeking. Showcase your talent on social networks when appropriate. Sharing your knowledge helps you become a mentor and, in turn, find mentors.

Most people go an inch deep and a mile wide with their conversations. This is what's most often referred to as *small talk*, as I mentioned earlier. We believe people don't go deep enough to really figure out how to make the most happen with their connections. That's what we suggest. Figure out what really matters to you and then do the same for those you connect with and, subsequently, through this *how-can-I-help-you* exploration, in return for giving and introducing others to new opportunities, you'll get introduced to new opportunities. My career has advanced further and faster because of my connections and so has Melissa's career. You can do the same. Soon your social networking success will begin to grow.

I grew up with few material possessions, little opportunity, and yet, even before I went to college, I valued connections. Why? Because everything that happened that was positive in my life was always a result of a connection that I made. Not everyone has had these experiences. Many people grow up with everything, or nothing, handed to them and it affects how they see life, how they network. But they can change.

I can remember an example as early as junior high. There was a youth worker from a program called Youth for Christ. His name was Rich Wood, and he was a minister. At first, I thought nothing of him; he was just a white man visiting our all-black school. But to the principal he said, "Hey, give me the kids who are a little wild and out there. I want to have them experience something different." I happened to be one of these young, wild kids. There were fifteen of us, all in the seventh grade.

Rich developed a relationship with us, and started telling us about Christ. He began exposing us to different experiences. He took us out of the inner city, and we went up to summer camp for a few weeks during summer. I became closer to Rich and accepted Christ at fourteen, after which I started to become a group leader. We took trips, including a ten-day canoe trip in the Porcupine Mountains in Canada. Another trip was driving to Yellowstone in Montana. At fifteen, no one in my family had ever experienced anything like this.

Rich gave us many new experiences. At the time, I reasoned that this opportunity was a blessing from God because I had accepted Christ. But even beyond that, my relationship with Rich was built on trust, whereas others, particularly black people in my neighborhood, were leery of him. After my first year, my younger brother became involved too. We'd hear people say, "Why are Billy and Michael involved in this and hanging out with this white guy? Why'd he come here?" Despite the distrust of my family and neighbors, I had to learn to trust and develop my own relationships. To this day, I'm still close with Rich, and he was there when I got my distinguished alumni award from Saginaw Valley.

A lesson Rich taught me early on was to have principles and to stick by them even in situations where you might waver. I had a girlfriend in high school, and we were voted "most likely to get married." We were together from ninth through twelfth grade. I ran track and played football; she was a cheerleader. But I was principled and held strong beliefs, and I remember there was a lot of peer pressure on me to do things that went against those beliefs. I wanted to be an example for my teammates. My girlfriend was very attractive and outgoing and many liked her, but one day in the locker room I said we were against premarital sex. To my buddies, it was a joke, along with my saying that I wasn't going to drink alcohol.

But, those were my principles in high school and I stuck to them. I credit my ability to stick to my principles with making me into a leader. I don't charge up to the front of the group demanding to be a leader. But because I'm focused, hold firm to what I believe in, and am action-oriented, people supported me.

Tips

- **Become a networking influencer.** You may not yet be at the top of your field, but because you're willing to practice influencing—connecting people who haven't met but who should meet—you can quickly become a top influencer, creating many opportunities for yourself. For example, you might know people in your industry who are highly influential but are not good influencer partners because they keep their power to themselves or confine their power to a small, insular group of colleagues. Their influence is actually limited because they don't understand how to be inclusive and diverse with their networking.

- **Study and model the successful networkers.** Treat all people as potential partners in networking. Your short-term objectives will keep changing, whereas your long-term ones will remain stable. Looking back, I can see that Rich influenced me tremendously. I was learning to network without even knowing it.

- **Realize that networking effectively is about building long-term relationships, not just collecting names and numbers in a database.** What you can't give today, you'd be surprised to find you can give tomorrow. Your intent to deliver is what really matters. As a proactive networker you'll find that you can create opportunities for your referral sources as you build a circle of high quality, rather than high quantity relationships.

- **Create three top signature success stories.** These are your stories that pass on both tacit and explicit knowledge about who you are and why others should care. Use these stories to build credibility, but, more importantly, connection with your contacts. If you have trouble creating your own stories, ask a colleague to interview you and record the interview.

Commencement

In the beginning of this book I told you that I would share what happened as a result of my conversation with my brother. Let me now take you back to it. When I told him how nervous I was about accepting the distinguished alumni award and revisiting my college years, he encouraged me to feel the fear and do it anyway because it was the right thing to do. I paused for a moment, letting his words soak in. Then I said, quietly, "You're right." I went to the ceremony and was blessed, humbled, and enriched by the experience, the award, and the people I met and talked with.

It's been five years since that award. A couple of years ago, I again received a call from Saginaw Valley, this time from the president of the university. I was in New York on business trip for Heidrick. I was hopping into a cab on my way to a client meeting as a partner with the firm. As he introduced himself to me, he commented, "I know you're surprised to get a call from me."

I said, "I'm surprised, but I'm also happy to get a call."

He got right to his request. "I wanted to see what you were doing on December 18 or 19? I wanted to see if you would be the commencement speaker for our 2015 graduates."

I was silent for what seemed like minutes.

He continued, "I wanted one of my most respected graduates to speak."

This time I didn't resist the honor. This time was different. This time I embraced my journey. After I got over the initial shock, I said, "This would be a personal highlight of my life. I would be honored to do this."

Once again, I was humbled by this strange, full-circle moment in my life. I had to tell my partners at Heidrick that I would be missing the yearly Christmas party, and told them proudly where I would be instead. My manager was very complimentary. It weighed heavily on me that he knew that side of me. As successful as I've been, I'm still protective of that side of my story. I've always wanted to be judged exclusively on the merits of my work, not on my past or my struggles.

I was totally unprepared for how he responded upon learning I would be speaking at the commencement.

He said, "Billy, there are three things that I always admired about you. First, I have never seen anyone develop as deep relationships and connections as you have with others. I know this journey through Heidrick has not been a bed of roses, but you have been joyfully resilient."

He continued, "Second, even when things have not gone your way, you stuck in there and continued to be a team player."

When he said this I couldn't help but see the other side, which was that often when others don't get their way, they leave. Well, sometimes I would push back, but when I came to Heidrick, I came in with a brand of my own. I knew when I came here I had to help them to know what my brand was *outside* of Heidrick. I pushed for leadership roles.

Finally, he said, "Third, you're one of the best people and nicest guys I've ever met." I didn't realize until that moment that our achievements rarely stand alone. They reach out and touch others. We learn from both our achievements and the impact our journey has on others.

His comments were an unexpected bonus to the honor I had been offered and it was humbling and amazing at the same time. Having the support and praise of your peers is incredibly rewarding.

But even as I prepared for this amazing moment, I had no idea of what it would mean to my life. As Melissa says, these are the unique connections that have given me the best direction to go and thrive. You heard about the honor, and the unique opportunity I had to give the commencement speech at my alma mater. Now, if you're like me, you might not have realized that the word *commencement* means *beginning*. I realized that this opportunity brought me another full-circle moment—to deliver the commencement address to over 10,000 people at the university that had initially declined my admission.

Melissa felt something similar to me when she was inducted into her high school hall of fame, being one of only forty-eight people out of thousands to be honored. The school now displays her picture and a commemorative plaque in its trophy showcase. This was the same school where shy Melissa had felt awkward and not as popular as her classmates. But she used her passion for connecting and helping others through networking to create a wonderful life for herself, her two sons, and her growing family.

Our focus for this book was to share our stories of struggle along with the lessons we learned along the way. We also wanted to share our *collective* strategies and tips to give you as many tools as possible to help you build your own nets that *work*. We also wanted to find ways to bless others with what we've learned, practiced, and developed throughout the years.

As we look at our evolution around this topic over the last twenty years, technology has significantly impacted what networking looks like. For some people, all they know about networking is associated with technology—Facebook, Twitter, and, of course, LinkedIn. These tools make networking more *efficient*, but they can't make networking more *effective*. There's still a huge need to pay attention to that high-touch piece.

This is probably a blind spot for me. But Melissa came up around the curve, writing almost a dozen books on the subject of networking both on and offline and investing years in facilitating events for all kinds of companies and organizations. She has also invested her time giving back in communities around the country and the world, ensuring they learn how to network as well. All along, similar to my passion, her main goal has been very simply to ... make a difference.

Whether you call it art or science or you have blended the two mindsets, it's all about making your net *work*. We hope that as you've read this book, you've found some ideas that you'll go out and try as early as tomorrow. Now, our greatest wish for you is this: pay what you've learned here *two-ward*. In other words, share your insights with at least two people. That way, you'll not only keep reaping the rewards of your knowledge, but also build a life that's meaningful and, most significantly, *make your* net *work!*

Before you go

Our main goal in this book was to provide you with that 20 percent of wisdom that yields an 80 percent return on your investment of time with the focus on growing making you net *work*. Our passion to others, like yourself, continues beyond this book.

Our doors are open for additional questions and support to help you realize the vision of creating successful and rewarding networks. To connect, please visit either www.billydexter.com or www.networlding.com.

Finally, if you liked this book—if it helped you even a little—please consider taking five to fifteen minutes and writing a review on Amazon that shares what you to write felt was most beneficial for you. Reviews make a difference for authors and we greatly appreciate, in advance, your thoughtfulness in taking the time to offer this form of support to us. Meanwhile, here's to your ongoing success!

ABOUT THE AUTHORS

Billy Dexter

Billy Dexter is a Detroiter who has spent half his adult life in Chicago. He is currently a managing partner at Heidrick & Struggles, a global leadership advisory search firm.

Billy grew up in a tough neighborhood on Detroit's west side with very few role models and low expectations for career success. Many would say if you just read the statistics his story should not have happened.

However, it did. What Billy had was passion and a strong sense of wanting a better life and to break the circle of poverty and no sense of purpose. He channeled his focus to get into college after many rejections and started his journey of making connections that developed into relationships that created many opportunities for Billy and those in his network. Billy serves on the boards of Link Unlimited, Executive Leadership Council, Metropolitan Club of Chicago, the Goodman Theater and the NFL Players Association. These represent Billy's many passions and together, make up a unique network in their own right.

Billy has been called a master networker and connector and has had a great corporate career that has taken him all over the world with United Airlines, Motorola, Deloitte, Monster Worldwide, Hudson Highland Group, Viacom/MTV Networks and, for the last eight years, connecting executive talent to major firms around the world at Heidrick & Struggles.

Melissa G Wilson

Melissa is president of Networlding and Networlding Publishing Inc. She is also the author of five bestsellers. Her latest book, *Networking Is Dead: Creating Connections that Matter*, was a *Wall Street Journal* and Barnes and Noble bestseller.

In 2009 Melissa started Networlding Publishing, for thought leaders who want to write books that make a difference in the world. She found that she could make the biggest difference by following her Power of Ten networking process to help ten to fifteen authors successfully write, publish, and launch their books yearly.

Over the last six years, Melissa has taken her twenty years of experience in publishing to help one hundred authors successfully write, publish, and launch their books. Her clients have included people like the head of diversity for Hewitt, the president of Holland America Cruise Lines, the head of a division of Allstate, the director of human resources for the NBA, a seven-time *Inc.* 500 entrepreneur, and thought leaders from many small and mid-sized companies.

Melissa's greatest passion is helping young adults get better starts in their lives and careers. To this end, she recently started a nonprofit with 501C3 status called SparkStart (www.sparkstart.org). Here, she provides, at no cost, the opportunity for her authors to launch their make-a-difference books as mentoring tools for disadvantaged young adults to get better starts in their lives.

ACKNOWLEDGEMENTS

by Billy

To Melissa. Thanks for your friendship and helping me to stay diligent on the project. To all of my former colleagues who helped me develop strong connections to build my networks. To my mentor, George Frazier, who helped me to understand how to be a "connector." Also, thanks to Stedman Graham who helped me develop a personal brand strategy. Thanks to all of my "Circle of Friends" and family who have always supported me and encouraged me to "tell my story." ONE LOVE! Billy D

by Melissa

I'd like to thank the many people who have helped me learn and practice both the art and science of networking throughout the years. My thanks to Jocelyn Carter Miller for the many years of practice I received working with you both at Motorola and Office Depot.

A huge shout out to the University of Chicago Women's Business Graduate Advisory Board for the many years I was gifted the opportunity of working to help graduates learn and practice better networking.

To the many organizations that reached out to me to facilitate interactive networking events including these schools: Loyola, Northwestern, Wharton, DePaul and including these corporations: American Express, Accenture and Disney.

Finally, thank you to the many non-profits I was able to serve including the United Way, the YWCA, the YMCA and Make a Wish.

NETWORKING TIPS

Following is a list of tips that were in this book with additional, new tips as a bonus:

- **Start with what Melissa calls a Power-of-Ten Circle.** This involves building one-to-one relationships with ten or fewer people. These are people who hold similar values to you. They are great choices as networking partners. This is what I've done with groups like my Circle of Friends golfing group.

- **Set up regular gatherings with your circles of support, either one-to-one or as a small group.** By building consistent exchanges with your networking partners and circles, you'll create more opportunities for yourself and others.

- **Make some of your connection events fun.** Whether it's a play, a sporting event, a concert, or just going out for a meal. It's the social side of networking that helps grow business opportunities. Even if you're just starting out, ask someone you admire to meet with you and perhaps even become your mentor.

- **Set up regular gatherings with your circles of support, either one-to-one or as a small group.** By building consistent exchanges with your networking partners and circles, you'll create more opportunities for yourself and others.

- **Create one or two social media accounts.** If you don't have a LinkedIn, Google Plus, Facebook Business, or Twitter account, we highly encourage you to obtain at least one or two of these. Create robust profiles. In fact, LinkedIn, a professional network, say users with complete profiles are forty times more likely to receive opportunities through LinkedIn.

- **Start your own blog.** A general rule of thumb is that you should have at least ten posts addressing different subjects prior to sharing your blog in order to lend credibility to your effort. A blog enables your loyal friends and fans to consistently connect to you in a fresh and robust manner. Your blog should be your cornerstone for social networking, because it's of your own making and free of outside influences.

- **Join LinkedIn groups.** While you can join up to fifty groups, it's more practical to participate in six to eight groups and make your contributions meaningful. There are many topics to choose from and aligning yourself with your field of interest and industry should be easy. Ask insightful questions and provide informed perspective in discussions.

- **Don't become lazy about welcoming new followers online.** Interaction online is the name of the game. Take the time to look at your new follower's profile and ask them something about themselves or comment on something interesting you read about them in their profile. If you follow someone, do more than just ask to join their network. Take time to tell them why you want to join their page or group. Don't just settle for the standard, "I want to join your network" e-mail. Personalize your requests.

- **Follow up promptly after face-to-face meetings.** E-mail or call quality contacts you meet at networking gatherings promptly after an event to remind them of your initial meeting. You can even include your Twitter and LinkedIn when you reach out. Reserve Facebook for close personal contacts. Let them know you enjoyed meeting them. Focus on the appreciation you have for the original meeting and mention that you would like to stay connected. This is not a time to sell your services or products, but rather, a time to grow and deepen the connection around the relationship.

- **Stay in touch with your networking connections.** Build rapport and follow them on Twitter, connect on LinkedIn, and subscribe to their blogs. Maintain regular phone contact and e-mail with information of value such as upcoming events or groups or important industry happenings.

- **Grab a pen. Bring back the art of good written communication by writing thank you notes to all your old and new contacts.** Read trade journals in your industry. Find people who interest you and write to them using personalized note cards. Include an article you find online or in a magazine with a handwritten note at the top saying something like, "FYI, George. Thought you would benefit from reading this article! Warmly, Your Name"

- **Manage your networks using a tool such as Hootsuite, where you can integrate multiple accounts and schedule tweets and updates.** We understand you're busy, but avoid the temptation of utilizing automated "response" programs. If your participation in social media appears automated, your credibility will suffer. Provide for meaningful personal time in your daily schedule.

- **Curate content by choosing the best tweets, posts, articles, and other information (including your own best) and assembling it in one place.** Use a tool like Storify (which is especially good for interviews) and scoop.it (arranges it in a gorgeous magazine format). You'll be able to share them with your connections and establish yourself as a go-to person in your industry.

- **Network up and down.** When you network up you look for people who have influence in your industry or the community in general. These are the people with whom you can offer more connections of value as you meet people who they don't know but should know. Networking down is about being the mentor. Dave Ormesher, president of a great web-design and development company called closerlook, shared that he acquired a large account with a company because he had befriended and mentored one of their salespeople several years ago when everyone else would not give this person the time of day. Dave realizes that all people are worth the time it takes to let them know they're important and to provide them with guidance as to how to grow successfully.

- **Treat each person you meet with uncompromising respect.** Great networkers are zealots of respect and integrity. They're like the knights in King Arthur's roundtable. They care about creating relationships of honor.

- **Suspend judgment when you meet someone new.** We often find ourselves meeting people who, upon first glance, don't seem to have the wherewithal to exchange or just don't seem like the sharing type. However, we make it a rule to give each person the opportunity to exchange with us toward the possibility of partnership. I constantly mentor others toward becoming better partners. I see this as a way to teach the world through these people–how to be better at sharing. For instance, Melissa works with a journalist who was formerly homeless. Rather than focus on the "homeless" tag she looked past that, discovered the woman was a TED Global speaker and had connections at the top media outlets in the country. She was also a giver and a networker.

- **Be creative when thinking of people to contact.** Start with people who really like you and brainstorm with them. Get them to give you a few names of people they really like but for one reason or another you have never met.

- **Connect like-valued people and groups together.** This strategy is about you becoming the matchmaker. By being the connector you become that person everyone wants to know because you make things happen. It's people who create opportunities and because you brought the people together, you stand out as someone others want to know. In turn, opportunities will come to you.

- **Be selective. Don't just throw two people or groups together.** Make sure there are leaders in each group who will work collaboratively for the good of both groups.

- **Test out your artful merging of networks with a small event.** Through the years both Melissa and I have created events that have brought us ongoing new business opportunities. But we also took our time building the initial events that were small, manageable, and filled with those from our networks that gave us feedback as to how to improve the next time. We kept improving our smaller events until the bugs were worked out and we could scale them.

- **Stay with your formal networks to the point they're running smoothly.** In other words, be a good shepherd of each group.

- **Create a statement that tells others what you do in the most favorable way.** For example, an accountant might say, "I help people start and maintain small businesses by getting their financial business squared away."

- **Co-create opportunities that offer the biggest win for the greatest number of people.** Project collaborations, strategic alliances, and partnering opportunities are all examples of ways to leverage relationships for maximum gain.

- **Request a referral in one industry or company at a time.** People will more likely remember these types of requests. Why? Because they are more specific. Think about it. With as much information as we're bombarded with daily, it's hard for any of us to keep straight who asked us to help them let alone how we could best help them. This suggestion here of being more specific will go a long way help people remember your requests. Which leads to the next tip.

- **Become an active listener.** Listen for understanding versus listening for information. Your attention to your networking partner's needs and interests will help you create opportunities that can lead to even more and better opportunities for you in your networking exchanges.

- **Stay open to new ideas.** Appreciate the new information or different way of looking at things your network partners offer. Even if you don't agree with them, respect their opinions. Successful networking comes from being open to the different viewpoints and ideas others share.

- **Keep asking questions.** When you do the asking you can lead the conversation toward the most successful outcome and that outcome should be about both you and your networking partners gaining value from a networking exchange. Questions also keep both parties participating.

- **Create a list of the best questions for generating conversations.** Great questions set the stage for great answers. Great answers inspire. Think of the best questions you can ask to start great conversation and exchanges. For example, if this were the best year of your life, what's the one thing you would do?

- **Stay genuine.** Being prepared is great, but without sincerity, you have nothing. When you're genuine and sincere, you'll attract people to you who naturally want to help you. Become interested in others. Find out what matters most to them and then center your conversations around their priorities. Of course, you should also share your priorities and network with those who care what matters to you as much as they care about what matters to them.

- **Become a networking influencer.** You may currently be someone who is not at the top of your field, but because you're willing to practice influencing—connecting people together who have not yet met but who should meet, in turn, you can quickly become a top influencer. For example, you might know people who are in your industry who are highly influential but are not good influencer partners because they keep their power to themselves or confine their power to a small insular group of colleagues. Their influence is actually limited because they don't understand how to be inclusive and diverse with their networking—something that would benefit them as well as others.

- **Study and model the successful networkers.** Treat all people as potential partners in networking. Your short-term objectives will keep changing whereas your long- term ones will remain stable.

- **Realize that networking effectively is more about building long-term relationships, not just collecting names and numbers in a database.** What you can't give to your network today, you would be surprised to find you can give tomorrow. *Your intent to deliver* is really what matters. As a proactive networker you'll find that you can create opportunities for your referral sources as you build a circle of high quality, not high quantity relationships.

- **Continue to spend quiet time, regularly, looking at the makeup of your network.** As you take time and look at your network, you'll discover links connecting from where you are now to goals and potential people who could help you achieve your goals.

- **Create three top brand stories.** These are your stories that pass on both tacit and explicit knowledge about who you are and why others should care. These stories can be about someone who has helped you, or how you have helped others, or about how you learned a new networking skill. No matter what, it's good to have a written account that showcases the value proposition you can bring to your network.

- **Use your stories to build credibility and connection with your network.** If you have trouble creating your own stories, ask a colleague to interview you and record the interview. If you want, pay them something for the effort, or treat them to lunch or dinner.

- **Create balanced networking exchanges.** Life's lessons keep bringing us back to this truth. You don't benefit in the end when you take much more than you give. Here, you often end up with much less that you would have received if you had been more generous. The same is true when you give much more than you take. Here you wind up with little to show for your efforts.

- **Become a networlder.** A networlder, unlike a networker, has ten or fewer key people whom they consider partners. These partners regularly exchange emotional support, information, knowledge, promotional support, as well as leads and referrals for new business or career opportunities. The focus of networlding is on mutually beneficial exchanges with like-minded and like-valued people. The great thing about *Networlding* partnerships is that they're fun and get results three to five times as fast as traditional networking relationships.

- **Spend 80 percent of your relationship-building time with your primary circle.** We know this is counter intuitive this focus will make all the difference in achieving better business opportunities, faster. Of course, that doesn't mean you can't have a large secondary or even tertiary network as evidenced on LinkedIn.

- **Consider where you're currently networking.** Is there a special go-to place you have where everybody knows your name, like Cheers?

- **Remember to look for a quiet place where you can hear the other person**. If you have to raise your voice to talk your conversation and connection may be compromised. Just suggest, "Why don't we step over here to a quieter spot where we can hear one another better?"

- **You have only one chance to make a first winning impression.** Make sure you have set yourself up for success with where you choose to start and show up as your best self. Use the mantra "Be Here Now."

- **Allow serendipities to happen.** People may come into your life for a reason, a season, or a lifetime, but you don't strategically say, "I'm going to go out and look for this person."

- **Look at your career in three-year increments.** This strategy helps you to stay more focused. You don't want to stay too comfortable. Decide whether you want to stay on for another three years or move on from your current place of employment. What do you want to accomplish in three years?

- **Throw yourself a challenge**. Say you're good at marketing and sales. Explore groups where you focus on building other skills that are relevant. Here this may look like developing your technology skills.

- **Get visible.** For example, sit on a panel or volunteer for an in-house project that's not part of your daily workload or join a nonprofit.